Library of
Davidson College

CHOICE, CLASS AND CONFLICT
A Study of Southern Nigerian Factory Workers

HUMANITIES STUDIES IN AFRICAN POLITICAL ECONOMY
General Editor: Gavin Williams, St Peter's College, Oxford

This is a new series of scholarly books which seeks to present the results of recent work on Africa. It aims to publish clear and accessible writing which combines the results of original empirical research with a coherent exposition of general principle. Some titles will be written by political scientists, others by sociologists, anthropologists and historians. But all will inform other disciplines than their own and contribute to a more complete understanding of Africa's problems, its past and present development.

1 *Choice, Class and Conflict: a Study of Southern Nigerian Factory Workers*
  Adrian J. Peace
2 *Capital, State and White labour in South Africa 1900–1960*
  Robert H. Davies

CHOICE, CLASS AND CONFLICT

A Study of Southern Nigerian Factory Workers

ADRIAN J. PEACE

*Lecturer, Department of Anthropology,
University of Adelaide*

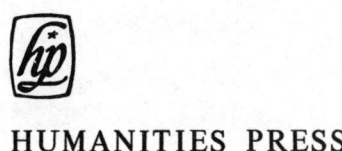

HUMANITIES PRESS

First published in the United States in 1979 by
HUMANITIES PRESS INC.
Atlantic Highlands, New Jersey 07716

© Adrian J. Peace, 1979

Library of Congress Cataloging in Publication Data
Peace, Adrian J
    Choice, class, and conflict.
    (Humanities studies in African political economy; 1)
    Bibliography: p.
    Includes index.
    1. Labor and laboring classes—Nigeria, Southern.
2. Nigeria, Southern—Social conditions.   I.   Title.
II. Series.
HD8831. Z8S686 1979   301.44'42'096691   79–12658

ISBN 0–391–01027–1

Printed in Great Britain by
Redwood Burn Limited, Trowbridge and Esher

All rights reserved

To my parents

Contents

Preface	ix
1 The Migrants and their Social Setting	1
2 Friends, Networks and Employment	21
3 Urban Careers and Self-Employment	49
4 Status and Class in Everyday Life	81
5 Unions, Leaders and Followers	109
6 Workers, Unions and Rebellion	139
Notes	177
Bibliography	193
Index	199

Preface

Throughout sub-Saharan Africa, young men from predominantly rural areas are migrating in ever-growing numbers to modern urban locations in search of wage-employment. The ramifications of this mass migration are considerable and complex. Notwithstanding the apparent ability of rural communities to adapt to the temporary or permanent loss of their youth, social and economic relationships within them are fundamentally and irrevocably transformed. In some established urban areas, an influx of migrants with their need for housing, foodstuffs and consumer goods, inevitably leads to major changes in local market relationships. In other metropolitan locations, existing facilities prove inadequate to cope with the growth of a wage-earning labour force with the result that new lower-class urban communities spring up, often exhibiting novel social forms with no evident precedent within the cities or the rural areas from which the migrants have come.

The impact is not merely limited to migrants' places of origin and present locations of work and residence. As more and more wage-earners are engaged in manufacturing a diverse range of consumer commodities, the use to which their labour power is put has consequences for the entire economic fabric of their respective societies. Moreover, by virtue of their size, their concentration, the relationship to the means of production and to the State, these new wage-earners comprise a significant force in the national political arena. Here is one element of continuity with the past for, as the course of the nationalist movement in colonial Africa well demonstrates, organized and unorganized labour played a distinctive role in winning political independence from Western Europe. With independence, this distinctive contribution has been enhanced rather than diminished since it is within public and private industrial enterprise that the oppressive bite of wider and increasingly unequal political relationships is most acutely felt and reacted against.

The processes set in train by the expansion of Africa's proletarian populations provide grist to the mill of several academic disciplines. History, economics, political science, and political economy, all have some part to play in accounting for their diffuse impact. The present study, although appearing in a series on African political economy, draws primarily on the research orientations and techniques of urban anthropology which, in sub-Saharan Africa, has made a particularly impressive mark, despite, or perhaps because of, its ill-defined academic boundaries. Social anthropologists have had considerable success in describing the variety of ways whereby migrant workers come to terms with the pressures of modern urban industrial life, and they have developed methodological techniques and sociological propositions of interest and application well beyond the research contexts in which they have been generated. I have tried to draw on some of these in order to bring out the richness of social life in Agege and Ikeja.

A preface seems an appropriate point at which to stress that a number of major changes have taken place in Nigeria since I conducted research there.[1] Regrettably, if understandably, the instability in the higher echelons of the political system has continued from the nineteen sixties well into the present decade. In July 1975, a *coup d'état* led to the removal of General Gowon and his military governors from power. In February 1976, a further attempted *coup* proved unsuccessful, although the then Head of State, General Muhammed, was assassinated and replaced by General Obasanjo.

Important developments have emerged in the relationships between the government, leading industrial employers, and the Nigerian working class. Most readers will be familiar with one innovation, the attempt to curb inflation by imposing a wage-freeze, for the Nigerian government is scarcely alone in the erroneous belief that curbing low-paid workers' wage-levels will stem the inflationary spiral inherent within contemporary capitalism. A further change has been for government and managements to move away from periodic reviews of general wage-levels, a pattern firmly rooted in the colonial era, to one of collective bargaining within the framework of a general incomes policy. The setting up of the Udoji Commission in 1974 indicated how difficult it was to make this break with the past, just as the furore which surrounded the Commission's work signalled how very necessary it was to effect such a break and to do so as soon as possible. The most important development, however, has been that, since 1977, following the report of the Adebiyi Commission[2] which was established to investigate the country's trade unions, the government has embarked upon a far-reaching reorganization of the labour movement. Its aim has been to sweep away the existing trade union system and to put in its place a single central labour organization with a restricted number of affiliates covering specified areas of industrial production.

In substantial part these changes are a direct consequence of some of the events described in the following pages. As will be seen, trade unions in Ikeja in the early nineteen-seventies were autonomous local level organizations led by democratically-elected shopfloor men, and they were fully geared to protecting the key interests of ordinary workers. Enhancing job security and improving wage levels were their *raison d'être*, and union leaders and their members were fully prepared to defend their collective interests. In doing so, they presented a severe challenge to those in power, and left no doubt as to their readiness to engage in further confrontation should occasion demand it.

The attempted reforms of the labour movement represent an unequivocal attempt by those in government to bring such local level unions within the orbit of state control to a greater degree than ever before. If successfully engineered, they may severely circumscribe the organizational ability of ordinary workers to defend their interests against policies imposed from above, and to articulate their deep-rooted dissatisfaction with the extent of inequality in Nigerian society. I have not had the opportunity to return to Nigeria since 1971 and so cannot describe the response from below to these government initiatives. However, the fact that those in power have acted with relative speed and decisiveness to restructure the trade union movement serves to confirm the importance of the events described in the final chapter of this monograph. Even as they occurred, it was evident to all that major developments were afoot. In retrospect, these were perhaps of greater significance than the workers, their leaders, or for that matter the present writer, were aware.

These remarks do more than reinforce the point that the pace of social and political change in Nigeria is remarkably rapid. They highlight some of the inherent limitations of an anthropological study, and suggest certain of the gains to be made from a closer working relationship between urban anthropologists and political economists. In this book I have tried to locate the analysis of the workers' circumstances and collective actions within a broader trajectory of change in Nigeria. Yet I am painfully aware of having mainly presented a series of snapshots of a local urban industrial landscape at a particular moment in time, and of succeeding only to a limited degree in relating the workers' actions to more general processes of political change. For these reasons, I would suggest, the interests of the urban anthropologist can be, and should be, closely wedded to the concerns of the political economist. While the former may modestly aim at producing accounts of a local situation, the latter must rely on an accumulation of these in order to specify the events and processes which show the direction of change in any society. Conversely, with the benefit of hindsight, and within the framework of general processual accounts of change, the political economist can help to set in proper perspective the importance of events which the anthropologist observes at first hand and which he endeavours to explain by drawing on actors' own accounts of their social situation.

It is, I believe, possible to go further than this and argue that the urban anthropologist should select his key problems for research from the work of political economists. Specifically, this means the work of Marxist political economists who, whatever their failings, have done most in recent years to uncover the structural forces bringing about social change within African nation states in the colonial and post-colonial periods.[3] This marriage of interests, however should not be such as to deny the anthropologist the opportunity to focus on the detail of day to day social organization which is one of his disciplinary trade-marks. In my own case, I lived with the workers whom I studied throughout my research period. Within my neighbourhood, I became involved in a range of local activities and developed a number of special friendships, some of which I have drawn on for detailed case material in this book. Through these friends, I developed a wider circle of acquaintances, among whom numbered several trade union leaders. Both sets of relationships were centrally important to later survey work, including a survey of my own locality, and one of the labour force of a prominent factory. My research, therefore, was methodologically eclectic, as such a location requires it to be. More important, had I not lived and worked in the manner associated with social anthropologists, it would not have been possible for me to present in detail an account and an interpretation of conflicts which are perhaps of particular interest to political economists.

The research on which this book is based was financed by a grant from the Social Science Research Council (U.K.) for the study of social stratification among urban Yoruba. From 1969 to 1972 I held a Junior Research Fellowship in the School of African and Asian Studies at the University of Sussex. To the Council, to the School, and to the University I am indebted for the generous facilities which they provided for me.

Throughout this three-year period, I was fortunate in having Professor P.C. Lloyd, of the University of Sussex, as my supervisor and colleague. It was from him that I acquired much of my training in social anthropology and learned most of what I know about Yoruba society. I am particularly grateful for the light hand with which he supervised my research and the tolerance which he showed as I made innumerable mistakes in the field and in writing up my D. Phil. thesis. I am equally indebted to Mr. Gavin Williams, of St.

Peter's College, Oxford, who with his customary enthusiasm and under difficult circumstances has edited the present manuscript with his wife, Gillian Williams. Since we were in Nigeria and Sussex together, I have long benefitted from his intellectual stimulus and generosity, and even though our political views may be somewhat disparate, I have gained far more from our conversations than he can be aware. I would also like to make special mention of Professor J.D.Y. Peel, of the University of Liverpool, who first introduced me to West African studies several years ago, of late commented on a draft of this book and in the interim proved a firm and most stimulating friend.

Whilst in Nigeria, I acquired a multitude of debts too numerous to mention here. It would however be most remiss of me not to mention by name my co-tenants Mr. Solomon Adetula and Mr. Nichodemus Mamah, and Mr. Patrick Noyin, all of whom guided me through the intricacies of Agege life and provided many insights into the functioning of the Ikeja Estate. In Nigeria too, Dr. David Lucas, now of the Australian National University, performed many kindnesses for my wife and I, including that of sharing his accommodation in Lagos when it was most needed. A chance contact with Dr. Paul Lubeck, now of Adlai Stevenson College, University of California at Santa Cruz, subsequently developed into another close association which I especially value. Since he was engaged in research among Hausa workers in Kano at the same time as I was working in the south, conversations with him always proved most rewarding.

For comments on drafts of the present study, I am much indebted to Dr. Cherry Gertzel of Flinders University, South Australia, Dr. Ralph Grillo of the University of Sussex, and Dr. Keith Hart of Yale. All three read drafts with numerous weaknesses but did so with understanding and a close attention to detail. The same qualities were displayed by Mrs Marion Crook and Mrs Ray Mulvihill who transformed my desultory efforts at typing into impeccable manuscripts.

My colleagues in the Department of Anthropology, the University of Adelaide, helped considerably in tightening up several chapters presented as papers to our departmental seminar. Their comments were all the more appreciated as most of them have interests at some distance removed from my own. To Professor Bruce Kapferer and Mr. Roy Fitzhenry I am most indebted for both have repeatedly made incisive and constructive criticisms, a number of which I have tried to incorporate into the final product.

My greatest debt is to my wife, Jane. Her contribution has been inestimable, ranging from assistance in the collection of data to managing our children single-handed as I wrestled with successive drafts. In a very real sense this is a product of both our efforts, and if this book is at all readable it is due to her. Finally, for myself I must thank the factory workers and their leaders who answered my questions and queries with infinite patience and tolerance, whilst on behalf of both of us, I record our gratitude to the people of Agege, and especially our neighbours in Morcass. Throughout our stay they treated us with a degree of generosity which quite defies description.

Adrian Peace

1 The Migrants and their Social Setting

This book is concerned with elements of the social organization of southern Nigerian factory workers who are for the first time residing in a modern urban setting and experiencing the deprivations of wage-employment. Most are young men who are recent migrants from the well-established towns and villages of the Yoruba kingdoms of south-western Nigeria. Their place of residence is Agege, an urban settlement with a population of 70,000 on the northern outskirts of metropolitan Lagos. They are employed on the Ikeja Industrial Estate which is adjacent to the Town and which has during the last decade become one of the most important concentrations of industrial manufacturing in Nigeria. On or near the Estate some fifty factories provide employment for about 18,000 workers. Roughly half of these live in Agege. The rest are residents of Lagos suburbs to the south. It is the former whose relationships are predominantly bounded within the Town and the Estate with whom I am primarily concerned.

In the course of the book I hope to make some contribution to two areas of study. The first of these is the social anthropology of African wage-earning populations. A number of important ethnographies have been published over the past three decades. Those which come most readily to mind are A.L. Epstein's *Politics in an Urban African Community*,[1] J. Clyde Mitchell's *The Kalela Dance*,[2] and Philip Mayer's *Townsmen or Tribesmen*.[3] Notwithstanding their concern with Central and Southern African migrants, these are seminal analyses of lasting relevance to anyone whose research focus is modern urban industrial life in sub-Saharan Africa. This is similarly the case with several essays written by the same three anthropologists and Max Gluckman.[4] More recent studies worthy of special note are two books by R.D. Grillo on East African railwaymen,[5] one by David Parkin on Kampala (Uganda),[6] Bruce Kapferer's analysis of workers in Kabwe (Zambia),[7] and an analysis of Zambian Copperbelt politics by P. Harries-Jones.[8] Other ethnographies might be added to this brief list. But the general prominence and excellence of East, Central and Southern African anthropological analyses can scarcely be disputed. By comparison we know relatively little about the social organization of West African wage-earners who have migrated to modern urban settings. Such studies as those by Michael Banton on Sierra Leone[9] and Margaret Peil on Ghana[10] help fill some gaps in our knowledge. Yet the outstanding omission continues to be Nigeria, although it has the largest wage-earning population in West Africa. I thus hope that the present study makes some contribution to countering this marked imbalance.

The second field of literature to which the book should be of relevance is the sociology of inequality and social stratification in sub-Saharan Africa. At the present time this is a burgeoning area of academic debate and deals with broad and wide-ranging issues. Common themes are social change in peasant communities, rural differentiation and stratification, patterns of urban development and conflict, the relationships between elites and masses, the role of the State, and contemporary patterns of underdevelopment and imperialism. By contrast with the anthropology of migrant wage-earners, in this sphere West Africa is rather well represented in the substantial range of books and articles. This is especially the case with regard to social inequality and stratification in Nigeria with recent contributions by P.C. Lloyd,[11] Gavin Williams,[12] P.C.W. Gutkind,[13] J.D.Y. Peel[14] and others. I do not intend to review this literature here. Suffice it to say that most commentators acknowledge the importance of Nigeria's small class of wage-earners to social and political change in the country, whether past, present or future. (This is made especially clear in Robin Cohen's invaluable *Labour and Politics in Nigeria*.[15]) Despite this consensus we do not as yet have a mono-

The Migrants and their Social Setting

graph which concentrates on Nigerian wage-earners as they cope with the exigencies of modern urban life and the demands of industrial employment in the context of a highly unequal society.

My aim therefore is to provide a fairly straightforward ethnography of the workers in the Town and on the Estate. I hasten to add that in no sense is this meant to be a comprehensive study. The economic, social and political realities of this migrant labour force are too complex for that. I concentrate on selected issues such as the circumstances under which workers come to the Town, the interpersonal relations they develop within it, their attempts to improve their circumstances, the organization and efficacy of their trade unions, and their political status in relation to their environment. Nor do I intend to make any generalizations from the analysis. The country's total number of wage-earners is relatively small, some 1.8 million or 6.4% of the total labour force and only 3.2% of the population as a whole, but the economic and social circumstances of this wage-earning class, which is widely distributed throughout the country, are enormously diversified. Moreover, the great majority of Nigerian wage-earners are employed by the State whilst the workers described in this book are in private employment. So even though the Ikeja Estate contains the largest assembly of factory workers in the country, a study such as the present one can be no more than a preliminary step in the direction of generalization and comparison.

This study is limited not only to a particular place, but also to a particular time. My research was conducted between August 1970 and December 1971 and for the most part it is to circumstances during this period to which I refer. This was a period of immense change in Nigeria. Only a few months had passed since the end of the Nigerian civil war. The military government was heavily involved in the task of economic and political reconstruction especially in the Eastern States. At the time my fieldwork began it was announced that military rule would continue for a further four years. The military government had made this decision mainly on the grounds that, in the light of their demonstrable inadequacies in previous years the old political class was incapable of negotiating the difficult transitional period between civil war and the re-establishment of a peaceful integrated state. There was much to be done: the reconstruction of the economy, further changes in and development of the twelve-state administrative system, the building of business confidence both within and outside the country, and the holding of a national census which had not been properly done since political independence. The military government considered itself best suited to meeting these challenges. Whether others did so was a moot point, though certainly in the ensuing months there were many rumblings of discontent not least from the ranks of the ex-politicians who, having been condemned to relative oblivion for the duration of the civil war, were now faced with a further four years out in the cold as a result of the continuing ban on political parties. There were more manifest signs of opposition, notably, in January 1971, a massive demonstration of discontent by a substantial section of Nigeria's low-paid wage-earners, including a majority of the Ikeja workers who are the subject of this study.

This event pervaded most of my time in the field. It occurred when I was about one third of the way through my research, and it was of tremendous moment for the workers. It arose through the government's having instituted a formal enquiry into the conditions of wage-earners at the lower reaches of the wage and salary scales in the country. The Adebo Commission (named after its Chairman) was instructed to make whatever recommendations it felt necessary in the light of the rampant inflation over the previous two to three years. One of its recommendations was a general wage-increase for all those on low fixed incomes,[16] and this the government accepted to the satisfaction of the Ikeja workers. A few days later, the government changed its stance in a remarkable fashion. It declared that certain categories of workers were no longer considered eligible for the Adebo awards, a ruling which applied to the workers in many Ikeja firms. The result was a successful rebellion on the Estate by the majority of workers employed there by West European managements heading local subsidiaries of multi-national corporations (for short, European companies). That success lasted with the

The Migrants and their Social Setting

workers for the rest of the year to the extent that scarcely a day passed without my having spent some of the time discussing the events with one or two workers. Thus, whilst any piece of anthropological research is the product of the immediate circumstances facing a given population, this is especially the case with the present analysis. This being so, most of the following chapters are written partly to account for the course of the 1971 disputes. Consequently I concentrate on the social organization of the majority of shopfloor workers who are employed in the European companies and who dominated events in the month-long crisis period. It is not a study of the strikes as such, but it is a study of workers who at the time I knew them had been involved in strikes which were of considerable significance. I shall not make continual reference to the disputes chapter by chapter. To do so would involve much disjointedness in the argument, but I would ask the reader to keep this development in mind.

The Local Topography

One elementary generalization which can be made of wage-earners in such diverse locations as Lagos, Kano, Zaria and Port Harcourt is that their involvement in industrial manufacturing is physically separate from other facets of modern urban life. In the location of this study, this is reflected in the distinction between Agege and the Ikeja Estate. This aspect of the local topography will be a recurrent one and is, accordingly, an appropriate point with which to begin the analysis. As can be seen from the accompanying sketchmap, the Town and the Estate comprise quite distinct physical entities. On the ground their respective appearances are strongly contrasting with Agege seeming the more interesting of the two locales.

In all, the Estate covers some 300 acres of land, a substantial area which is sub-divided into large plots. Each of these contains a single firm, all of which are production and administrative units autonomous from the rest. Broadly speaking there are two types of firms on the Estate. The predominant type comprises the European factories; these multi-national subsidiaries are the most technologically complex firms, and they are the largest, with labour forces of between 500 and 2000 strong. There are also what I will term the non-European companies, managed as they are by Taiwan Chinese, Lebanese, Syrians, and Indians; their employees generally number between 50 and 500. There is little in the way of co-operation between firms, in part because they produce quite different commodities. These include textiles, furniture, asbestos sheeting, paints, foam mattresses, tyres, processed foodstuffs, bottled beer, household enamelware commodities, and electrical equipment. Most firms therefore have different requirements from the rest, and since they are under different ownerships and management, they have little to do with one another, as is reflected by the physical boundaries of ditches, roads and barbed wire fences which mark out their different territories.

The factories provide no accommodation or leisure facilities for their employees. They are exclusively geared to the process of industrial production, and this results in the separation of employees' work experiences from other aspects of urban life. One consequence is that the Estate appears an arid and dismal place. Walking along Oba Akran Avenue, the major road on the Estate, or the other minor roads which separate factories from one another, one sees only low-lying buildings and perhaps a handful of workers moving around within each industrial compound. The only other signs of life are a few street traders selling cigarettes, sweets, soft drinks and cheap foodstuffs. Except on the main road these men and women are few and far between, and even they depart the scene during the hottest hours of the day. At such times the Estate is an especially depressing place. Its monotonous appearance is briefly disturbed with the change of shifts on which the majority of workers are engaged. Around 6 a.m., 2 p.m., and 10 p.m., there is a flurry of activity as the change-over is effected in all the factories at the same time. Small Volkswagen buses and other passenger vehicles suddenly fill the Avenue for a period of ten to fifteen minutes. No one lingers long on

The Migrants and their Social Setting

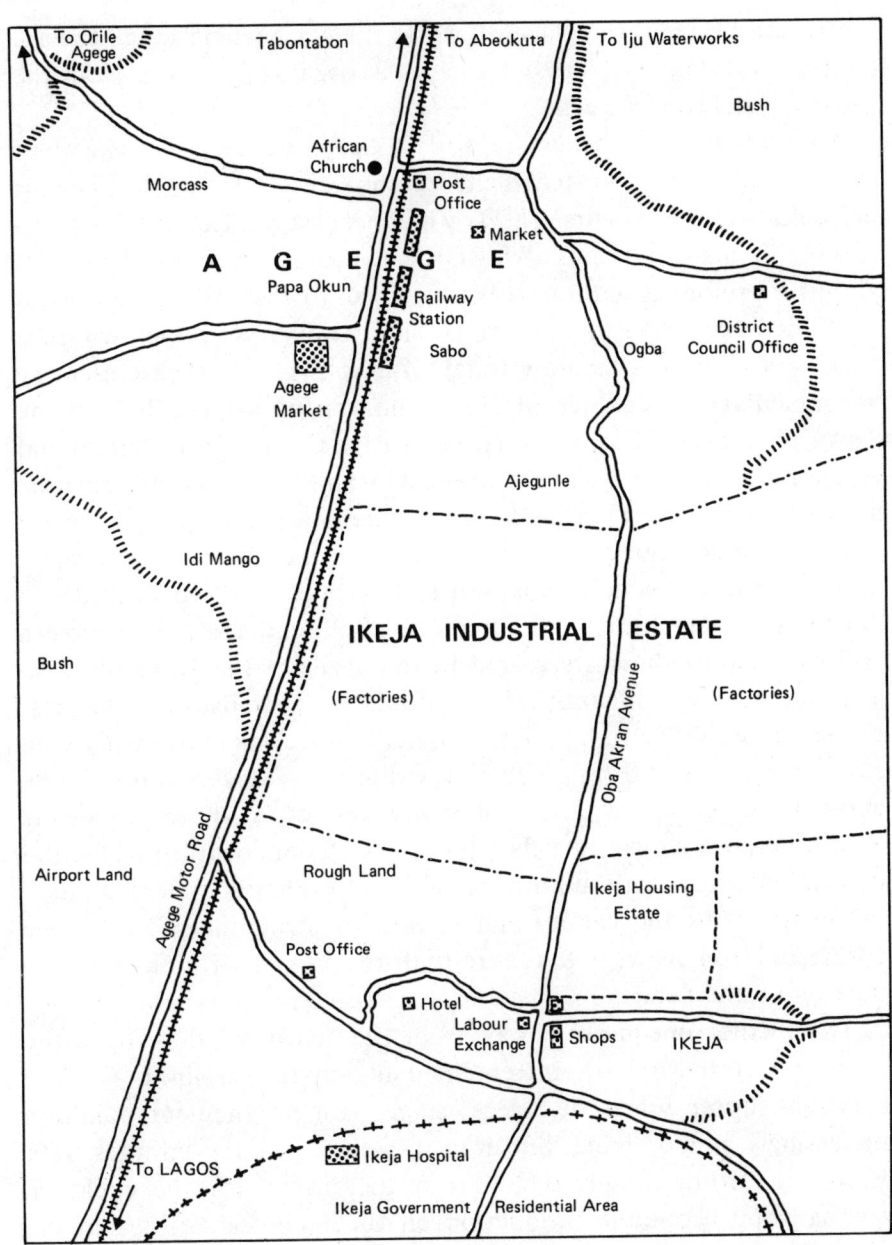

Sketch map of the Agege-Ikeja location

the Estate: 'Ikeja is the place we work, the place where we go to earn money. Nothing else. Once the shift is over we get away from the place as quickly as we can'.

About half the workers return to Agege where they take their leisure and reside in tenement rooms rented from the Town's indigenous entrepreneurs. The Town appears as a different world and so it is in many respects. Whilst the Estate is carefully planned in grid-like fashion, as with most West African townships, Agege has not developed according to any formal plan or design. In has grown since 1900 and continues to grow today in *laissez-faire* fashion presenting an immediate appearance of chaos and confusion. The hub of the Town comprises the oldest quarter of Papa Okun, Agege Market and Agege Railway Station. This area is a constant hive of entrepreneurial activity, particularly in and around the Market during the early morning. In addition, for about half a mile on each side of the Agege Motor Road — which runs south to Lagos and northwards to Abeokuta — are located hundreds of small shops, stores, canteens and bars. All of these are geared to the needs of the Town's heterogenous but predominantly poor population. Foodstuffs, clothing, household equipment, liquid refreshment, as well as more costly consumer goods, can all be purchased within a few dozen yards of one another. So too can a variety of urban services: at the centre of the Town, barbers' shops, bicycle repair sheds, tailors' workbenches, and carpenters' workshops are intermingled with other commercial establishments. Thus the variety and vitality of economic life at Agege contrasts strongly with the more uniform process of industrial production on the Estate.

The further one moves away from the centre of the Town, the more the intensity of entrepreneurial activity declines. On the sprawling outer limits of Agege, single storey tenement buildings increasingly predominate, but even these are only ten minutes walk from the Motor Road. By contrast therefore with the exclusive emphasis on economic production on the Ikeja Estate, within the Town there is an intimate juxtaposition of economic activity with all other forms of urban life. Buildings for business enterprise are found alongside urban residences in virtually all the Town's neighbourhoods. Entrepreneurial activity and residence frequently occur under the same roof. So one is never left in any doubt that the economic and social climate is set and dominated by the independently employed men and women engaged in a myriad of ways, making a living. As a result the minority of wage-earners spend much of their time when not at work in the company of traders, blacksmiths, bar-owners, carpenters, seamstresses, electricians and others, as well as that of their fellow factory workers.

Agege then is by no means a mere proletarian dormitory town. And as we shall see it would be mistaken to separate out the factory workers from those who are not wage-earners: their very co-existence is central to understanding aspects of the wage-earners' social organization and their aspirations for the future. Similarly whilst the townspeople are predominantly poor this description cannot be allowed to obscure or underplay the relative wealth and in some cases outstanding affluence of a minority of men and women in the Town. Poverty is the common lot and so too are miserable living conditions. There is a lack of basic urban services in the Town, most people do not have running water, many houses lack an electricity supply, adequate sanitation facilities are few and far between, and scattered throughout the Town are open rubbish dumps and fetid pools and ditches. Most tenement building rooms are poorly furnished with cheap beds, tables and chairs. Agege people generally own little more than a range of personal clothing and a handful of cheap consumer goods, and the factory workers share in this general impoverishment. But within any neighbourhood in the Town there also reside the owners of tenement buildings who, beside being urban landlords, are particularly successful transporters, storeowners, contractors and traders. These are invariably self-employed men and women who occupy profitable economic niches in this highly commercialized urban community. Whilst our main concern is the factory workers, we shall have to return to these people, some of whom are appropriately termed Big Men, for they are important points of reference to the factory workers.

The final elements of the local topography which require note are the Ikeja Housing Estate and the Ikeja Government Residential Area to the south of the Industrial Estate. In two respects these are of some importance. The first is that they are superior residential areas containing the houses of some of the most prosperous and powerful members of Lagos society. This is particularly the case with the Government Residential Area where residences of mansion-like proportions, Mercedes cars, and other trappings of wealthy bourgeois life-styles abound. For the factory workers at Agege this is the nearest representation of the vast gulf between their life-styles and life-chances and those of military leaders, politicians, prominent businessmen and senior bureaucrats in the Lagos metropolitan area. Second, the workers' own employers, both expatriate and indigenous managers from the Industrial Estate, generally reside in one or other of these two residential areas. Thus to the separation of work (at Ikeja) from non-work (at Agege) has to be added the complete segregation of the wage-earners in general from those who control and direct them within the factories.

The Migrants and the Themes of the Book

This then is the social setting: on the one hand the Estate where the factories provide employment for the migrants, on the other the economically and socially heterogeneous community where the workers live. Some of the above features will be returned to later. But this outline is sufficient for the moment to introduce the migrants and some concerns of the study.

There are several characteristics shared by the migrants which are of general importance. The first of these is that they make up a predominantly youthful labour force. The majority are in their late 'teens or twenties. This is almost universally the case for the shop-floor workers in the European firms who are my central concern. Only the small number of supervisory posts are filled by older men, most of whom are in their thirties or forties. Second, most young migrants are educated, though not to a high level. Virtually all have

The Migrants and their Social Setting

completed primary school, and a sizeable proportion have spent between one and three years in secondary school. The education of most has been prematurely terminated through lack of family finances, for the costs of secondary schooling are high (whilst primary schooling in western Nigeria is free) and most migrants are the sons of poor farmers or urban craftsmen and traders. Third, the migrants are relatively recent members of this modern urban industrial milieu. The Ikeja Estate was founded only in 1960 and the first expatriate companies, then with small labour forces, began production some two or three years later. Thus a small minority of factory workers have up to seven or eight years experience behind them. The majority of jobs on the Estate have, however, been created within the past four or five years following the expansion of existing firms and the setting up of many new ones. It has been the chance of taking up one of these newly-created posts which has attracted the young men to Agege and Ikeja. Most have gained them without any prior experience of wage-employment.

Fourth, the migrant wage-earners comprise an ethnically heterogeneous population. The great majority are from the traditional towns and villages of the Yoruba kingdoms of southwestern Nigeria.[17] These kingdoms have undergone markedly different patterns of historical transformation and change. In consequence, their internal patterns of structure and organization vary widely as do their respective populations' dialects, customs and other cultural forms. These differences continue to be of importance in categorical and interpersonal relationships between workers whilst resident at Agege, one manifestation of which is for migrants to classify themselves and others as Egba, Egbado, Ijebu, Awori, Ibadan, Ekiti, Ijesha and so on, according to the particular kingdom of origin. (By contrast only a very small percentage of workers are of non-Yoruba origin).[18] The fifth characteristic of the migrants is that they are relatively poor urban residents. According to my own survey material some two-thirds of the workers receive from their employers between £N10 and £N15 per month with most of these being at the lower end of this income range.[19] Certainly this means that their annual incomes are higher than the average of about £N50 for the population of western Nigeria as a whole. However, the recurrent costs of living in the Lagos metropolitan area are high: in 1970–1971 the basic requirements of accommodation and food were subject to very considerable price increases. Since the basic wage of £N10 per month was established in 1964, and even at that time appeared only just adequate for the individual single worker to meet his basic needs, by 1970 many migrants to Agege were finding it difficult to make ends meet. At all events these migrant workers do not enjoy the relative prosperity of many of their counterparts in East and Central Africa.

The final shared characteristic of these young wage-earners is that on migrating southwards they have considerable aspirations to advance themselves by finding employment at Ikeja and taking up residence in the Town. In fact it is important to emphasize that before moving to the metropolitan area of the capital, they have had several choices as to the careers which they will pursue on leaving school.[20] The most common occupation of the migrants' fathers is that of farmer. As such, they could have exercised their rights to use lineage land. This has certain attractions, notably a high degree of personal independence. On the other hand, even in the relatively prosperous but now declining cocoa-belt, the economic return is low considering the effort which farming requires. On these grounds this option has been turned down although many migrants' age peers have taken it up. An alternative to farming has been to become apprenticed to an urban craftsman or trader in the long established towns of Yorubaland. Although they are mainly the sons of farmers, most migrants have been brought up in such towns as Abeokuta, Ilaro, Ijebu Ode, Ado Ekiti, Shagamu and Ode Ondo: these are the capital towns of the Yoruba kingdoms and urban conglomerations in which reside predominantly farming lineages whose members commute to their land several miles away. Accordingly on leaving school young men have had the personal connections to arrange (or have arranged for them) an apprenticeship under a craftsman, trader or other urban entrepreneur. This has certain drawbacks: one is that a

The Migrants and their Social Setting

young man must continue to live amongst the members of his family and within his natal compound. At the same time such apprenticeships can be an initial stepping stone to social mobility within present-day Yoruba towns. Again some migrants' fellow school-leavers have taken up this option. The third option has simply been to hang around for some time in the hope that financial circumstances within their families will improve to the point at which they might return to school. Many migrants have in fact done this. But it is not a tactic which can be sustained for long. Finally the option has been to migrate and this of course is the one which has been fully embarked upon.

There are, however, three particular considerations about their having made this choice. The first is that it has often been made on the basis of partial or incomplete information. The second is that migrants come to Town in anticipation of considerable improvement in their personal circumstances over and above their home-town lifestyles. They expect some short term material advancement and the opportunity to enjoy the good things of modern urban life. The third is that more often than not young migrants anticipate spending only a few years in factory work before attempting to become independent or self-employed entrepreneurs. In contrast with, for example, some Southern African target workers who intend after a short period of wage-earning to return to their places of origin,[21] or some East African workers who anticipate entire careers as wage-earners,[22] these West African migrants approach factory employment in a different instrumental fashion. They hope to save sufficient capital to establish themselves as self-employed entrepreneurs in the longer run. They do not have a very clear idea as to how long they will remain factory workers nor as to how much capital they will require to establish their urban businesses. Nonetheless the aspiration to become self-employed is a near-universal one on the shopfloor of the Ikeja factories. Of necessity it is an issue to which we will return several times during this study.

In summary, we are concerned with a young, ethnically-mixed, somewhat inexperienced body of literate wage-earners who have only relatively recently entered the urban industrial setting of Agege and Ikeja. They are also, for the most part, ambitious young men who are concerned to extract the maximum possible advantages from their choice of involvement in this social setting. These potential gains they consider to be, in the short term, enjoying some material benefits from migration, and, in the long term, saving from their wages as a preliminary to economic independence. These are the distinctive qualities of this particular West African wage-earning population.

Equally important, however, is that as wage-earners they have much the same class situation as factory workers in Western Europe, the United States and other African capitalist settings. The migrants have only their labour power to place at the disposal of their employers. In return for low wages they must allow themselves to be directed into whatever role or task which managements require of them. To this extent their labour power becomes, under their employers' control, a commodity which like any other basic productive resource is to be used in order to maximize production and profit. Moreover, whether they are skilled, semi-skilled or unskilled, these wage-earners have no control over the nature of the commodities which they produce: nor do they have any degree of control over the disposal of the goods to which they have contributed their labour.

To put it another way, whilst there are certain features which distinguish the Ikeja wage-earners from workers in other capitalist contexts, there are basic aspects to their class situation which they share with any other proletarian population. One needs to be sensitized to both sets of factors and develop one's line of analysis accordingly. Some anthropologists and sociologists have argued that a class analysis is inappropriate as an analytic perspective for understanding social and political processes in African settings. The present writer believes to the contrary that a form of class analysis is quite essential and this will be argued throughout the book. So let us turn to some of the concerns which will be elaborated in the following pages.

The Migrants and their Social Setting 15

Of the five subsequent chapters, the first two are primarily, though not exclusively, given over to the description and analysis of aspects of the workers' social organization in the Town. The remaining three are concerned with their organization on the Estate in relation to their expatriate employers and also the government. This is merely a matter of convenience. It is not to suggest that the physical separation of Town and Estate must be matched by an analytical separation too. Quite to the contrary, in sociological terms the two systems of relationships within these physical arenas are interrelated and articulated in several important ways. The most general is that the expansion of the Estate from 1960 to 1970 has substantially contributed to the phenomenal growth of Agege: throughout the last decade the Town's population has more than doubled to the present total of 70,000. Moreover the expansion of entrepreneurial opportunities in Agege has been closely related to the growth of the Estate. Some of the more prominent entrepreneurs of the Town have come to the fore by taking full advantage of the opportunities generated by the factories. A notable case in point comprises leading Agege traders who are economic brokers between the Estate and the Town: they purchase large quantities of manufactured goods which they then break up into smaller quantities for resale in the Market and elsewhere. Passenger bus owners and building contractors have likewise benefited since they are profiting from meeting the migrants' (and others') need for cheap transport and housing. Some of these are the Big Men of Agege and whilst they stress the personal expertise, the entrepreneurial skills, and the good fortune which have made them wealthy and prominent, they will also acknowledge that their successes are closely tied to 'the coming of the factories'.

Of major relevance to this study is the degree to which aspects of the nature of workers' employment on the Estate ramify out into their domestic and other interpersonal relationships in the Town and give these relationships much of their essential form and content. The central aspects which are of significance are the low wages which migrants receive for their labour and the high degree of job insecurity which most face. These are critical issues for all the more recent migrants to Agege and they cannot change them as such. They have to adapt to them. They do so by adjusting their interpersonal relationships over which, of course, they do have some control and into which they can build a high degree of flexibility. The major feature of their social organization in this respect is the heavy reliance on small tight-knit networks of home-townsmen between whom a strong degree of trust and sense of mutual obligation exists. The nature of these social networks is described in Chapter 2: here I also outline the reasons why most recent migrants gain relatively little in material terms from their early involvement in this urban industrial milieu.

In Chapter 3 I examine somewhat different issues, the efforts of a minority of workers in the European-managed factories to realize the ambition to become self-employed men, and the ways in which these efforts influence their interpersonal relationships. As I have indicated, migrants generally come to the Town with the ambition of economic independence well established in their heads. These ambitions are greatly reinforced by the distribution of wealth and prestige at Agege which, in turn, are products of the articulation between Estate and Town. The focus of Chapter 3 is to indicate how exceedingly difficult and generally unsuccessful are workers' attempts to realize their ambitions. Indeed it will be argued that having voluntarily chosen the career of wage-employment with a view to longer term self-employment, the migrants are being involuntarily trapped in the industrial system in a fashion which heightens their feelings of resentment against that system.

In Chapters 4, 5 and 6, a recurrent concern is workers' patterns of adaptation to the dominant cleavage throughout the Estate between employers and employees. Notwithstanding the many variations between factories, in all companies the same structured opposition of interests between managements and workers underpins ongoing relationships. My aim is to describe the different forms of expression of this opposition. By way of introduction to this, the first half of Chapter 4 outlines the situation of my main subjects, the shopfloor workers, in relation to other wage-earners, the skilled workers and white-collar employees. Here I will indicate that the straightforward cash-nexus which binds the shopfloor men to their places of employment is to be contrasted with rather more complex ties between non-shopfloor men and their employers. At the same time I take it as axiomatic that the common class situation of all wage-earners finds overt expression in interpersonal and group relationships. Thus in the same chapter an attempt is made to show how all workers are engaged in the elaboration of a specific proletarian culture in which they express a sense of unity with one another and in opposition to employers. The manner in which their class experience finds expression in the course of everyday life is presented as essential background to more overt and noteworthy manifestations of workers' opposition to their employers.

The labour movement on the Estate is the subject of Chapter 5. In substantial part the chapter is taken up with an analysis of its strengths and weaknesses. Its strengths derive from the trade unions being restricted to individual factories: one product of this restriction has been for popular shopfloor workers to emerge at the leaders of the house unions, another is that these men are especially responsive to the concerns of the majority of ordinary members. The house unions are also, within some limits, effective organizations run on open and democratic lines. This may come as some surprise to readers acquainted with the now voluminous literature on African trade unions. As Richard Sandbrook and Robin Cohen have written: 'Most studies of internal union politics (in Africa) have rediscovered or confirmed Robert Michel's famous "iron law of oligarchy." '[23] This is not the case with the Ikeja house unions and an account of their functioning is therefore of some comparative significance. More important in relation to the present study is that in recent years the house unions have done a great deal to improve the circumstances of their members with the result that the workers have a strong commitment to realizing their interests through existing institutionalized channels of class conflict at the local level.

The Ikeja labour movement nevertheless has its endemic weaknesses, most notably its highly segmented form, the manner in which it is divided up into individual unions. In Chapter 5 we will also discuss the ramifications of such segmentation and the reasons why this has not yet been overcome. The major ramification for the workers is that the unions are not able to combine together in order to gain any degree of political efficacy beyond the level of the Estate. By 1970 it had become evident to union leaders and followers alike that some form of political representation towards the government was essential if even their limited life-chances were to be sustained. Particularly at this point of the analysis it becomes necessary to relate developments at the level of the Estate to changes in the wider political environment. This same orientation is carried over into Chapter 6, in which my aim is to locate the Ikeja workers in a wider political perspective, and to assess their political status in the context of the wider class system. I do so by reference to the events of January 1971 when the Ikeja workers and others were engaged in a major conflict with their employers and the military government.

It is in the above respects that this book is a basic ethnographic description and analysis. In analytic terms the Town and the Estate are approached as local level arenas in which specialized organizational forms emerge as workers combine on either an interpersonal or group basis in order to come to terms with the problems posed for them by their class position at Ikeja and their circumstances as residents of Agege. At later stages of the study I bring into the analysis important extra-local factors which are of especial significance for changes and developments at the local level. Since these are migrant workers, from time to time I also consider the nature of their continuing connections with their places of origin. Finally by way of introduction, it merits emphasis that the workers' unnatural relationship to productive processes within the Ikeja factories is greatly heightened by its contrasting with the relationship of self-employed men at Agege to the commodities which they themselves produce and often also dispose of. This contrast is one which is recurrently referred to by the workers and helps explain a number of their responses to wage-employment as we will describe them in subsequent chapters. One example must suffice here. It occurred in a small group of factory employees when one worker picked up a metal bowl and commented that the same morning he had had to purchase this item at Agege Market, despite the fact that as an employee of the enamelware factory he had most likely produced it himself a few days previously. He commented: 'What possible sense is there in that? Would a tailor make a shirt for sale only to buy it back later from someone else? We would consider mad a carpenter who made a table only to buy it back later from another man. But we factory men do this all the time.' He was being mildly humorous whilst he made this impromptu remark. Yet it is a revealing comment which must not be lost sight of, for it drives home how incongruous and invidious factory work can appear to those who constantly have on tap, so to speak, a qualitatively different system of productive relationships in which they would fully prefer to be involved. To draw on a well known remark concerning industrial employment: it adds to their abasement and their indignation at that abasement.

2 Friends, Networks and Employment

The major concern of this chapter is to describe how, in the context of the Town, the majority of recent migrants come to terms with common and critical problems raised for them by involvement in the modern urban industrial setting. This requires us to focus on the migrants' involvement in different types of interpersonal relationships in the Town, and in particular in personal networks of hometownsmen which comprise young men who have migrated from the same Yoruba town or its rural environs. On the whole, their trade unions apart, the migrants do not belong to large formally-organized associations or institutions at Agege or Ikeja. Their reliance throughout is on highly personalized dyadic relationships, an emphasis which gives a distinctly atomistic quality to their patterns of social organization. As indicated in the previous chapter, my main concern is with shopfloor workers in the European factories on the Estate. But as will become evident, the issues dealt with here are such as to make necessary inclusion of workers in the non-European firms. In whichever type of firm they are employed, the circumstances which face most recent migrants are such as to give much the same form and content to their interpersonal relationships in the Town.

We should first note that Agege people in general eschew membership of organizations and institutions of any substantial size. This applies to the majority of self-employed men and women in the Town quite as much as it does to the young factory workers. In this respect the community contrasts strongly with the social organization of many other modern urban centres in sub-Saharan Africa. A number of social anthropologists have pointed to the proliferation of ethnic or home-town associations,[1] neighbourhood societies,[2] religious brotherhoods,[3] community action groups and such like, in somewhat similar situations. By contrast, large voluntary associations at Agege are few and far between and draw in only a small proportion of the community's members. For many people their only affiliation with an association of any size is to a church or mosque, and these are usually quite small. In this respect too, Agege stands in marked contrast to the established urban centres of Yorubaland: within these, lineage associations, market traders' groups, craft guilds and other institutions are numerous and wide-ranging in their memberships.[4]

There are a number of reasons why this should be so in the Town at large. For a start, by Yoruba standards Agege is a new town: it is a product of the colonial period having developed around a railway station constructed at the turn of the century. As such, unlike most Yoruba urban settlements, it has lacked the pre-colonial institutions which elsewhere often flourished in adapting to the colonial situation and then retained momentum into the post-colonial period. Second, the population as a whole is ethnically heterogeneous in the extreme and ethnicity did not get built into the economic structure of the Town. Rather than there having developed an overlap between economic interests and ethnic categorization, members of the same ethnic category have become spread through a variety of occupations and economic niches, thus removing a potential source for the mobilization of large segments of the population. Third, the majority of self-employed townspeople have migrated, as with the young factory workers, over relatively short distances. For example, a large proportion are from in and around Abeokuta, the capital of Egbaland, which is less than a couple of hours by road from Agege: and even more distant places of origin such as Oshogbo, Ilesha, Ado Ekiti, Ondo and Akure, can be reached within three or four hours. So most Agege residents can retain close contact with their places of origin thus in part obviating the need for ethnic associations. Other factors might be added to these. But by far the most important influence is that the Town's self-employed men and women are engaged in highly competitive and individualistic ways of earning a living. In the last twenty years economic activity has boomed and the market for all types of goods and urban services has expanded enormously. In order to maximise on the opportunities created for capital accumulation, self-employed people must be flexible, innovative, and opportunistic: in short they must be risk-takers. In accordance with these requirements they must in turn cultivate extensive networks of personalized relationships with suppliers, journeymen, apprentices, clients and customers. This is not therefore a favourable economic context for formal rule-organized relationships to flourish and prosper. The stress throughout is on competitive individualism and this emphasis Agege people in general carry over into other spheres of urban life.

The Problems of Factory Employment

Turning now specifically to the migrant factory workers, their stress on informal interpersonal relationships is also related to the structure of the economic order from which they derive their living, in their case the Ikeja Estate. There are other considerations. For example from the time of arrival in the Town, personal ties are very important to any migrant: in order to gain a preliminary foothold in the urban situation a migrant must have acquaintances, for there are no bureaucratically organized avenues of introduction such as exist in some Southern African settings. Moreover, as young men frequently claim, the Town is 'a dangerous place' with many hazards and pitfalls for the unwary. To these factors we will return. Essentially it is the shared conditions of employment within the factories which give migrants' interpersonal relationships much of their form and content, most especially in the degree of reciprocity and the concern with trust which characterizes them.

The first main influence is that of workers' low rates of pay. As we have said, most migrants have only been in Agege for up to four years and some for periods considerably shorter than this; (of more established and better-paid workers we shall have more to say in the next chapter.) Their monthly incomes of between £N10 and £N15 are insufficient for any degree of personal security and stability in the Lagos metropolitan area. A worker attempting to live by himself on such a wage is forced to practice the most extreme forms of urban subsistence activity: few attempt to do so. Even with an income of £N15 an individual worker has little leeway for negotiating difficult periods in his urban career and some margin is necessary, as we shall see, for a migrant's continued well-being in this setting. In other words, low wages require substantial economies to be made on a regular basis and these are best achieved by workers pooling their slender resources.

The second major influence is that of near-endemic job insecurity amongst young migrants, coupled with the difficulties of finding employment in the first instance. There is a labour exchange to the south of the Estate and some unemployed youths register there, but most expatriate employers do not utilize its services, since it is (reputedly) slow, inefficient and manned by corrupt officers. Instead most hiring takes place at the gates of the Ikeja factories so that any unemployed youth ('an applicant' in local parlance) requires support from others whilst he seeks work, and personal guidance as to which factories he should hang around. Having gained some form of employment, a migrant's problems are by no means at an end. Three further substantial obstacles arise.

First, all workers are taken on by all Ikeja employers on a casual basis. They are paid daily or in some instances weekly. And during the next three months they can be laid off at any time. Since casual workers are frequently hired by their employers for short term tasks, this means that many workers drift from factory to factory with a few days in employment in one, a few weeks in another and so on. It is by no means uncommon in the Town to come across workers who have been in this situation for six months, a year or even more, with no immediate prospects of improvement or stability. Most shopfloor workers' careers include at least several weeks casual labouring after arrival at Agege. Throughout these periods, the migrants receive only the minimum wage; sometimes part of this has to go to the foreman in charge in order to ensure that they will be hired for more than a day or two.

The Nigerian government has no objection to this system of casual labouring, but it is required that after three months in casual employment, workers are transferred to the firm's permanent payroll. One effect of this is that many casual workers are sacked prior to the three month deadline. Once this point has been passed however there is a contrast in policy between factories. This gives rise to the second source of insecurity amongst recent migrants. On the one hand, in companies under the control of European managers, to reach the list of permanent employees does make a marked difference to the status of the migrant. He has a particular job allocated to him and he is relatively well protected by his house union. He remains on the minimum wage-rate for some time, at least six months and sometimes a year depending on the firm in question; but he is nevertheless secure. On the other hand in non-European companies this is not the case, mainly because these firms do not allow trade unions to function within their boundaries. If a worker in such a firm should as much as declare an intent to form a house union, then he is sacked, and external labour organizers are always refused access to these unorganized labour forces. In consequence, even though after three months a worker may be allocated a particular job (let us say on the production line as opposed to manual labour around the factory compound), there is no security of employment and workers are often 'terminated' for quite trivial reasons. The further point to be made is that recent migrants tend to become concentrated in these non-European firms. Because of the somewhat better conditions in European factories the demand to gain employment within them is always very high. This allows them to be especially selective in their choice of employees, and one of the points of selection is some previous wage-earning experience on the Estate. The more recently arrived a migrant then, the more likely he is to be stuck in a non-European firm and, therefore, the more insecure his position.

Many chance factors influence in which particular Ikeja firm a migrant gains employment and so it does happen that a few recently arrived ones find work in European companies: over time, more are able to move into these after a spell in a non-European firm. It is because of these chance factors that migrants' personal networks frequently contain a mixture of European company and non-European company employees: as such we must here discuss the two categories of workers together. The final feature which adds to the difficulties facing all wage-earners is that they must pay a bribe to factory personnel managers in order to be kept on after three months. These men have the power to determine who should continue in employment and who should not. If a worker cannot pay the bribe, then he will be laid off. In 1970 the going-rate for being retained on the shop-floor was £N10 with some variation according to particular firms. Since as a casual worker a young migrant cannot have saved such a sum, he must rely on others to help him pay the bribe.

So, to summarize the problems facing recent migrants: it is difficult to gain employment in the first place, all receive low wages, most face considerable insecurity in their employment, they have to pay in order to retain a job. All these problems are compounded by the hazards of urban life, including at the very beginning of their urban careers, establishing a foothold in the Town. After noting the self-evident point that the problems specifically created by employment are greatly to the advantage of Ikeja employers, we can turn to how the nature of migrants' interpersonal relationships helps them come to terms with some of these difficulties.

Elders, Friends and Brothers

An appropriate starting point is the problem of initially entering the urban milieu. Strictly speaking this is not negotiated by the migrant: usually it is handled by his father or an older kinsman. Migrants' parents are of course especially concerned about their sons' welfare in Lagos: to most of them it seems an extremely hazardous place. Accordingly they do not grant their sons permission to move southwards until an older host has been arranged. This role is filled either by a kinsman already resident at Agege or by a personal friend of a migrant's father or older relative. It is the availability of such a mature host which in part influences why a migrant arrives at Agege rather than any other of the lower-class suburbs of Lagos such as Mushin, Bariga or Ajegunle further south. Some workers say that they would have preferred to go to one of the suburbs of Lagos proper, usually for prestige reasons since amongst their home-town peers Agege does not have quite the same cachet as Mushin for example. They were prevented from doing so since no host could be arranged elsewhere.

Since the major function of a host is to provide accommodation for a migrant, usually he is an entrepreneur-landlord. As such he incurs few costs from having a young guest under his roof. Indeed some of these Elders (as they are regarded by youths) play out this role of urban gatekeeper on a regular basis: in the space of a year some have three or four young men pass through their residences. They do so in part because this enhances their prestige and personal reputations in their places of origin. They become known as men who are concerned about the welfare of young men absent from their natal households. These reputations will stand them in good stead when they retire home, as they invariably intend, and perhaps make a bid for a lineage title or more important position.

As a result, Elders develop a continuing interest in young guests and this is important to the latter. Not only do they receive free accommodation and food for a limited period of time, they can also turn to Elders later for other forms of assistance, such as a loan, should the resources of others fail. In some cases Elders can arrange employment: an Egba businessman in my own neighbourhood counted as one of his best friends an Egba foreman on the Estate and in one year placed three young guests within his factory. Migrants also encounter occasional bother with their landlords, with girl-friends' parents, with neighbours and the like. An Elder's social standing can be called upon to cope with such situations. Finally, an Elder can help out when a young migrant finds himself in dispute with his parents and other relatives at home. For example, after a few years migrants frequently come under pressure from their parents to marry. The modern urban experience of an Elder can be drawn upon to explain, on equal terms, why it would be precipitate for a wage-earner in Lagos to do so. In other words, after providing him with his first stopping place in Town, a migrant's initial host subsequently becomes a valuable ally who can be turned to on a variety of occasions to negotiate Town-specific problems as these arise. This then is the first set of interpersonal relationships in which migrants are involved. As we shall see, these relationships can pose difficulties where young men build up a range of material and non-material debts to Elders, but for the most part they are valued dyadic ties which are kept in good repair by regular visits well after migrants have left their hosts' houses.

The second set comprises friendships with fellow migrant workers, the majority of whom are from the same home-town or at least the same Yoruba kingdom as the migrant himself. These frequently number a dozen or score. They are fellow ethnics since, for example, a migrant from Abeokuta will generally count amont his friends Abeokuta men or others from Egbaland, a migrant from Ode Ondo will usually have as his friends migrants from Ode Ondo or rural Ondoland, and so on. The individual comes to know these men in two ways. Either they are friends from pre-migratory days, particularly ex-school friends who have preceded or followed him to Agege, or they are fellow townsmen encountered at Agege, since two men from the same place of origin, but with different circles of friends, will make a point of filling the gaps in each other's spheres of acquaintance. One result of this is that where the total number in Agege from one Yoruba kingdom is relatively small, then one migrant may know most, if not all, of them. This is the situation with migrants from Ode Ondo and the Ondo kingdom who number in total less than fifty. Conversely where the total number runs into several hundred or more as with those of Egba origin, even the most sociable migrant will know only a few. Whichever is the case, relationships between fellow townsmen are easy and relaxed, predicated as they are on the assumption that fellow townsmen whilst abroad (as being in Agege is regarded) should establish harmonious and cordial relationships.

Shared ethnic identification does not, however, necessarily create a sense of mutual obligation between fellow home-townsmen. The intensity of these dyadic relationships is highly variable. It is only from some of these that an individual migrant can expect material assistance should he need it. When he is in dire need as a result of the inadequate resources of his personal network a migrant will turn only to those for whom he has done some particular favour beforehand. Furthermore, whilst in general migrants count as friends a preponderance of home-townsmen, this is not to suggest that they are in any sense encapsulated or cut off from non-townsmen.[5] The general preference is for the former since they speak the same Yoruba dialect, share certain common cultural traditions, have overlaps in their past experience, and a common interest in home-town affairs. This does not rule out migrants developing friendships with those from the other Yoruba kingdoms: they frequently develop interethnic friendships, usually with factory workers and young self-employed men as a result of residence within the same tenement buildings. Through common residence some limited degree of reciprocity develops over time and this, whilst being limited, may be sufficient for a migrant to draw on when he encounters hard times.

This said, all migrants are quite emphatic that one's friends whatever their ethnic origin are of a qualitatively different order to one's 'urban brothers' in Town, these being the third and most important set of relationships, and the ones on which migrants are greatly dependent for support and assistance at all times. It is through relationships between urban brothers that the major obstacles to individual well-being are met. These are appropriately described as personal networks characterized by the dense and multiplex relationships existing between the members at any one moment in time.[6]

There are several basic characteristics to these social networks. They are relatively small. The norm is four or five although they range from between two and eight strong. They comprise fellow home-townsmen on the whole: only occasionally do networks comprise migrants from two ethnic categories and very rarely more than two. The ages of network members are generally about the same as is the length of time they have been migrant wage-earners. Members' wage-levels are usually much of a muchness. Rarely does more than five pounds separate the highest from the lowest paid: more often than not it is a matter of only two or three pounds. In brief, migrants' social networks are relatively homogeneous social units.[7]

A further feature of these networks is that members reside in the same tenement room or, if it is somewhat larger than most, two rooms in the same building or proximate ones. This brings us to the first major function of social networks. They enable their members to effect economies and they operate in such a way as to relieve at least some of the pressure on factory workers resulting from their low wage-rates. In this respect shared residence is especially crucial. The majority of tenement rooms in the Town are rented out at between £N3 and £N6 per month depending on size, the age of the building and its location. If migrants were to live singly then the cost of accommodation would be quite crippling, roughly half to one-third of their monthly incomes. This would leave quite insufficient money for meeting other necessary requirements month by month. By 'packing' (i.e. overcrowding) tenement rooms with three or four migrants then the cost of rent is kept to a relatively low proportion of their monthly incomes. It should be immediately stressed that this is not necessarily to say that this releases money for surplus or non-basic expenditures. Frequently all it means is that the members of a network can make ends meet on a regular basis, whereas were they to live singly or even in pairs they would not be able to do so, such is the disparity between the minimum wage-level and the costs of purchasing basic necessities in the Lagos metropolitan area. Through joint residence of this kind further economies are made possible in the purchase of foodstuffs, kerosene for cooking, electricity and water.

So this is one respect in which urban brothers are different from friends in the Town at large. Brothers are fellow home-townsmen who pool factory wages on a regular basis in order to purchase basic necessities. As indicated, such a pooling of incomes frequently means that workers can just get by in the Town whilst under other circumstances they would not be able to do so. At the same time networks can and do generate some slight degree of joint income surplus. It is difficult if not impossible to say under precisely what circumstances networks simply make ends meet as opposed to their having a little money in hand at the end of the month. Several features bear on this: the size of the network, the personal (external) debts of individual members, the number in the network with incomes slightly over the minimum wage-rate, as well as the number out of work. All that can be asserted is that most manage to generate some surplus from time to time and that this is mostly used in the support of members in difficulty. This brings us to the second major function of migrants' networks: they are support units which allocate available surplus finances in such a way as to come to terms with insecure conditions of employment on the Estate.

Note that we are talking here of only small and irregularly-generated amounts of money. They are not marked surpluses: for the most part it is only a matter of one or two pounds per month, rarely more than three or four. Moreover only under rather particular circumstances (detailed below) do they arise on a regular basis. To have money in hand in several successive months is simply not possible within most migrants' networks: instead the pattern is for no excess income in one month, a little in the next, and so on. This of course is because networks must carry unemployed members on a recurrent basis. Over the space of let us say six months or a year they find themselves supporting one or more of their members following the loss of positions in non-European firms and/or interim periods of unemployment between casual labouring jobs. In other words as joint income surplus arises it is fully committed to negotiating a period of hardship faced by an individual member: it is used to pay his share of the rent, his proportion of food costs and the like. It is also stored up in order to pay the necessary bribe with a view to his gaining more permanent employment, should he be offered it after three months casual work.

It should be added that it would be easy to overstate the amount of planning which is made in preparation for periods in which network members have to carry a colleague. Equally however the time at which extra finances will be required can be predicted somewhat in that migrants taken on as casual workers quickly gain some notion as to whether at the one extreme the work will last one or two days, or at the other, possibly lead to a more permanent position. Network members can prepare themselves for certain likely contingencies in the relatively near future. Some illustration of these points will be given in a moment. For the present the important consideration is that a good deal of trust and mutual understanding is necessary for this support function of networks to be effectively realized. In so far as small income surpluses are being generated, so they are all the more valuable considering the low incomes of recent migrants. Members have to operate on the basis that the individual currently being supported will reciprocate in due course when others encounter similar difficulties to his own. So in what way is such trust created and reinforced over time? There are two aspects to this: how individuals gain membership of their networks and how a network's capacity for looking after its members is repeatedly tested.

I have already indicated that at the beginning of his urban career a young migrant typically resides with an Elder whose presence at Agege is an important reason for the youth being in the Town rather than elsewhere in Lagos. But this is only a part-explanation. Quite as important is that a young man already has at least one close friend in the Town. Usually this is a particularly intimate friendship formed in primary or secondary school and then kept up on the occasion of home-town visits made by the first member to migrate. On such visits too, arrangements are made for the second to follow. After residing briefly with his Elder-host, the new migrant moves into the tenement room of his close friend and the latter's existing social network, amongst whom the decision has already been taken to help the new arrival. With these others he may have some degree of prior acquaintance, but effectively the new migrant's close friend vouches for him. More than this, a kind of implicit bargain is struck between the new arrival and the members of the network as it currently stands. By allowing him to join them they are also committing themselves to using their various resources to provide him with accommodation and food, and also assist him into work. To put it another way from the start the basis for a degree of trust is being laid. Over time this modest starting point is elaborated and reinforced.

Subsequently new migrants undergo what might be loosely termed a *rite de passage* in order to legitimate their status as dependents. For example, one firm expectation of any new arrival is that he will assume most of the daily household chores for the entire residential unit. Similarly it is expected that he will make a point of establishing relationships with a wide circle of fellow home-townsmen through whom information about available jobs can be picked up. Most important is that a new arrival must assume the exacting task of waiting each day at the gates of Estate factories on the off-chance of gaining casual employment. It is through these performances that the new man gains acceptance by the rest. By tackling all such tasks diligently the new migrants demonstrate that they are worthy of the initial assistance provided by the others: they show in effect that they are good fellows who merit membership of the group. Thus when they have the opportunity of gaining more permanent employment, the other network members feel reasonably confident in deploying their surplus income to his personal advancement. They consider that by paying the bribe necessary for a factory job, they are fully incorporating into their ranks a new member who will subsequently reciprocate when someone else in the group encounters his own difficulties. This is a somewhat oversimplified picture which will be revised later. But in rudimentary form this is the process whereby most social networks have built up their composition of four, five or more members. The individual has initially been drawn in by virtue of intimate friendship with one member and via a vetting process gained full membership. It is in effect a rudimentary process of incorporation and co-optation with the final stage being the point at which the new member, once fully employed, reciprocates *vis-à-vis* others and demonstrates that their trust in him has been well placed.

The second process which encourages mutual trust and understanding is a corollary of the first. As time passes the material and non-material resources of any migrant network are continually being tried and tested by numerous incidents which strengthen the degree of reciprocity within the group. On a day to day basis members are constantly involved in some degree of minor reciprocity: most things are shared, ranging from food, packets of cigarettes, to clothing, household equipment and the like. But the resilience of a network is fully tested by the recurrent incidence of unemployment. An instance of unemployment, particularly when it is handled successfully using only the internal resources of the network, contributes substantially to the on-going continuity and solidarity of the social unit, the more so as the experience is repeated.

For example, during the course of a year, I followed the changing fortunes of six such networks which ranged in size from two to seven members. Only one of these, the smallest, avoided an incidence of unemployment. Two networks (of three and four members) carried one colleague for periods of ten weeks and five months. Three groups (one of two members, the other two of five members) carried at different times two unemployed members for periods ranging between four weeks and five months. The largest network which was seven strong experienced three incidences of unemployment which lasted three weeks, eleven weeks and three and a half months. Under such circumstances as these, therefore, the mettle of migrants' networks is constantly being tested. The critical point is that while it may be onerous for those in employment to assist 'an applicant' recurrently, they do so willingly even for lengthy periods since they act on the assumption, as they must, that they may find themselves in similar circumstances in the relatively near future. A strong element of self-interest thus underpins the manner in which recent migrants support their less fortunate fellows. This being so, it is of no small comfort for the currently employed members of a network to see an unemployed one back in work once again, even though their accumulated income surplus has been quite exhausted. Not only are they free from the financial burden of supporting him and now have a further income to add to the general pool, the resilience and reliability of the social group have been proven and indeed reinforced in such a way that they too have a good chance of surviving a spell in the ranks of the unemployed. In addition, the financial ramifications of one incidence of unemployment may carry over for some time since it frequently happens that in order to pay the bribe for work, the income surplus of a network must be supplemented by cash loans from beyond the group. Although they have been raised by an individual member from his Elder, a friend or a landlord, the repayment of such a loan becomes a joint responsibility.

Continued co-operation, a complex set of reciprocal exchanges, and a high degree of mutual trust are, then, the main characteristics of recent migrants' networks. Accordingly migrants say that urban brothers, as opposed to mere friends, trust one another, they are generous with one another, and that between brothers everything is shared. These are the elements of the ideology of urban brotherhood which migrants constantly expound. Material debts such as the observer might record are not closely calculated by the members of the network. This applies to small recurrent expenditure, quite as much as it does to major outlays such as those necessary to secure employment. It is assumed that constant pooling will in the longer run work out into a position of rough and ready equivalence and it is understood that to be concerned about balancing out such transactions would make impossible the functioning of the group. Finally the ideology of sharing rests on the assumption made by members that it may be their turn next to lose their jobs. In the words of one migrant:

> If you treat your brothers like other townspeople (i.e in relation to debts) then you will be quickly lost. Brothers are the only people you can trust at Agege and if you are not generous with them then you will not survive. If there is no money at the end of the month, you have to work together to survive. If there is money left in your pocket, then it is not yours alone, it belongs to your brothers as well.

Managing Instability

So the migrant has three crucial levels of support: the Elder who has assisted him in the past and can continue to do so in the present, a wide circle of friends, and his urban brothers with whom at all times insecurity and instability are to be jointly confronted. These varied social relationships can be drawn upon in different combinations in order to manage a variety of Town-specific and Estate-specific problems. An appropriate case study concerns Tunde, a nineteen-year-old migrant from Ode Ondo who over some months found himself in several difficult situations. The relationships on which he drew were those with his Elder-host, Obi, his senior sister's husband and the entrepreneur-landlord with whom he first lived, and Henry and Jose, both of whom were home-townsmen and old schoolfriends at whose suggestion he had migrated to Agege. But Tunde needed the support of others too.

On arrival at Agege, Tunde took up residence with Obi until he found casual work in the same firm as Henry. Henry had advised him that the foreman of the factory would be recruiting labourers on a particular day. Shortly afterwards, he moved in with his urban brothers who loaned him the money to buy a mattress and a few other necessary items. Three months later the resources of the network, supplemented by small loans from outside it, were used to retain his employment in the Chinese-managed enamelware factory. At roughly the same time he ran into trouble in the Town. A young rice trader in the Market short-changed him and in a brief scuffle she fell and cut open her arm. In the outcry, Tunde ran away; but since the girl knew him slightly, her father in the company of a policeman went to his tenement room and then, finding him absent, to Obi's house nearby.

At this point, the connection with his Elder proved invaluable for the youth was hauled before the Town's Native Court. Before the Court, Obi spoke in favour of the young man and explained his actions on the grounds of his inexperience in Lagos and his natural petulance. Obi had performed in a similar capacity on several occasions previously and he knew personally one of the court judges. Tunde was fined £N10 for disturbing the peace, a sum paid by his Elder. The latter further insisted that Tunde personally apologize to the father of the girl and pay him a couple of pounds from his own pocket. With this Tunde complied.

His next difficulties, by contrast, were negotiated through membership of his personal network, but not before some changes had occurred within it. Largely as a result of several petty disputes with Jose who had come to consider Tunde as touchy and immature, Tunde moved in with Saka, likewise an Ondo man and a close friend to all three network members. After a brief interlude, cordial and reciprocal relationships became established among all four. Next, their resources were considerably supplemented with the arrival of Michael, a close acquaintance of both Henry and Jose, despite his having resided beforehand in Mushin. He was already permanently employed in a European-managed firm (and was thus the most job-secure of all) and wished to move closer to his workplace. To this end he moved in with Henry and Jose.

So the network had expanded to five-strong and it was this social unit which functioned as a safety net for Tunde, when five months later he was sacked, and entered into a thirteen-week period of unemployment. Notwithstanding his minor differences with Jose, all his urban brothers considered him to be fully one of their number. The major contributions to his rental payments came from Jose, Henry and Saka. He also received several small sums of money from half a dozen Ondo friends outside his immediate social circle. The most important aid, however, eventually materialized through Michael having joined the network. The factory in which he was employed began taking on temporary employees as manual labour for the construction of new buildings. By giving a small bribe, Michael had the foreman in charge of hiring take on Tunde from the ranks of the unemployed at the factory gates. Three months later, using a sum of £N10 which had been carefully put together during that period by the network, Tunde was able to pay the necessary bribe to the factory's personnel manager for a permanent post.

This is to describe in bare outline, the more notable experiences of one young migrant over the space of some eighteen months. One feature of importance is the slightly changing composition of the network during this period: this requires us to modify the earlier picture of network emergence which, as was noted, is somewhat oversimplified. Notwithstanding a considerable degree of continuity, networks do change in various ways. They draw into their number home-townsmen already at Agege and known initially as friends to existing network members. This results from the dissolution of other networks: Saka for example had lost the other member of his previous network when he had moved to a factory at Apapa Port. The status of friends therefore is transformed into the status of urban brothers but only where, as with Saka and Michael, the existing members feel that another is a valuable asset to the group and where it is felt that he can be fully trusted. As the account shows, Michael in particular much merited the expectations which others had of him.

But taken in its entirety the account points to how a young migrant can negotiate, or perhaps be negotiated through, a difficult period. His informal relationships with Elders, friends and urban brothers, provided they are carefully maintained, can prove sufficiently flexible and adaptable to existing circumstances as to prevent the migrant going under, so to speak. Because of the variable statuses of significant others the individual is able to draw on varied resources in order to negotiate Town-specific obstacles or those emanating from the Estate. Obi the Elder proved an invaluable ally in meeting the difficulties raised through residence in the Town. By drawing on his status as an older man presumed by others to have authority over wayward youths from the same home-town as himself, he contributed to Tunde getting off rather lightly from his appearance before the Native Court. As we have indicated, relationships with a wide circle of fellow home-townsmen are on the whole considerably less complex than those with brothers. Yet they entail some sense of shared responsibility. Thus Tunde received several small sums of money from certain of these when he was unemployed. And finally, it was through the multiplex relationships which Tunde had with the members of his network that he was supported through the lengthy period of unemployment. Whole-hearted assistance was accorded to him by these young men. On previous occasions he had helped them: for example when Henry had had to return home on the death of a senior kinsman, Tunde had contributed to a pool to finance Henry's trip. When his own 'time of trouble' emerged, then support for him was quite spontaneous. Especially in raising the bribe to gain permanent employment in a European company, they helped Tunde to emerge from this difficult phase in a relatively comfortable position. Although his wage was the minimum of £N10 per month, by becoming a permanent worker within this company his position was considerably more secure than that of most recent migrants. It is in this fashion that the young migrants are able to come to terms with the particular and general problems of living and working at Agege and Ikeja.

Home-Town Visits and Clubs

So far I have been concerned to describe the most basic advantages which derive from network membership. There are also certain secondary advantages which are enjoyed by the members of some networks.

To repeat an important point, recent migrants' networks generally comprise a mixture of employees from European-managed firms and non-European ones. Because so many random factors influence the type of company in which a migrant gains employment, it frequently happens that a network of four or five contains one or two workers in European company employment whilst a larger network still may contain more. Their presence is of importance to other members because, though in the first instance they are employed on the minimum wage-rate, they have relatively secure jobs and they come under the protection of their house unions. More than this, over a year or two, they move away from the minimum wage level as a result of annual increments and increases realized through house union pressure. Provided that other members of these networks are not unemployed for lengthy periods of time, then all can begin to spend a bit more freely and to enjoy some of the benefits of modern urban life. This may not last for long: it can be quickly brought to an end by a single member losing his post or by a newly arrived migrant joining the established network. Both of these can easily occur. Nevertheless, under these somewhat restricted circumstances, workers can realize some compensation for previous months of deprivation and difficulty. Such periods of time are of course much prized by recent migrants: the opportunity to have some finances for pleasurable activities is one of the main reasons why they have migrated to Agege. Before migrating most have had no independent source of income: they have been entirely dependent on their fathers and, at best, have received only small sums for their personal use. Generally, their personal possessions have consisted of no more than a few items of clothing.

Where the above conditions are met, then there are several ways in which surpluses of income over necessary expenditure are used up. The first of these, as one might expect, is in the purchase of clothes and other cheap consumer goods. Young Yoruba males are exceedingly concerned about their personal appearances. So, on an individual basis, they spend much of their money on the purchase of ready-made shirts and European-style trousers which are cheaply produced by the large number of young self-employed tailors resident in Agege. Alternatively collective purchases are made of somewhat more expensive consumer items for generalized use within the network, in particular pieces of furniture and electrical goods. For those who can afford, an electric fan is the usual choice: only rarely do funds stretch to the purchase of a second-hand bicycle. After clothing however, the most common way of spending small amounts of money is on visits to the local cinema or to the local photographer for pictures which are framed for display in tenement rooms or sent home to parents.

Income surpluses are also taken up by making home-town visits. One point of comparison to be made with accounts of wage-earners in other parts of urban Africa is that the majority of recent migrants considered here are not engaged in the sending home of regular remittances. They well know that, faced with recurrent obstacles to individual stability and security, they simply would not be able to keep these up. Instead migrants undertake visits to their homes and these are timed to coincide with particular events such as a wake, a naming ceremony, a kinsman's marriage or the marriage of an old school-friend. As with more expensive consumer item purchases, these are generally co-operative endeavours: members of an Agege network return home in tandem, each confirming the others' status as fully-fledged 'Lagos men'.

Finally, and perhaps of most interest, an important, though not invariable, sign that a network of migrants is operating above the border-line is that they constitute themselves into small clubs. The term 'association' would be far too grandiose a label for these. Club formation entails not much more than a minor formalization of existing close-knit interpersonal relationships. A network assumes a particular title, some of which are as revealing as they are attractive: the Abeokuta Aspirants' Society, the Ever Ready Boys' Club, the Rising Stars of Egba, the Ijebu Self-Improvement Society. Each member assumes or is accorded a particular title: President, Chief Whip, Third Secretary, Second Treasurer. A monthly contribution of a few shillings is raised from members in order to purchase soft drinks or a few bottles of beer for consumption at weekly or fortnightly meetings, usually on a Saturday afternoon. The clubs are of consequence to any established network for they are especially manifest representations of the intimacy existing between members. They are indicating to others that they consider themselves a distinct unit of true brothers and that they have found their feet in the modern urban setting by virtue of their co-operation and trust. Particularly significant is that at certain times of the year, such as Christmas or the end of *Id el-Fitr* (the month long Islamic fast), they hold small ceremonies which are preceded by the accumulation of savings. On such an occasion, it is considered essential to have at least one older townsman as the special guest. This is usually the most wealthy and well-known Elder with whom network members are connected. Invitees also include members of other networks with whom they are particularly well connected. The expenditure is as much as can be afforded in order to meet the costs of food and drink and group photographs are the order of the day. The major outlay is always in the purchase of matching sets of Yoruba-style outfits made from the same roll of cloth. Thus the unity of the group is in various ways being firmly represented to others with the stress on their oneness and continued co-operation.

This is likewise the case with regular club meetings. Conversely these are sometimes used as an appropriate forum for sanctioning members whose actions have not appeared to be in the full spirit of urban brotherhood. The most extreme example I encountered took place within a group of migrants from Abeokuta. This network, which numbered eight in all, contained one youth who had received considerable financial assistance from the rest when he lost his job and when he had returned home for the funeral of the head of his lineage. Then for no apparent good reason, he abandoned his network and switched his allegiance to another quite unconnected with the first. This was considered quite reprehensible and so the Morning Star Society of which he was the vice-president, took action against him. One Sunday afternoon in his absence he was removed from office and ejected from the society, a formal separation which strikingly demonstrated the sense of grievance felt by his urban brothers of earlier days. But this was not an empty gesture. Not only was he informed of the action taken against him, word also reached (or rather was made to reach) members of the small group which he had joined.

I do not know whether this had any further repercussions, and this *was* an extreme case. Parenthetically, however, it allows us to note one important attribute of even the vaguest acquaintance which members of different networks have of one another. Through the transmission of gossip and scandal they may serve to keep in line those within them. This is even more so with established secondary friendships between members of different social networks. Since members of the same unit often have similar interpersonal connections beyond it, if a member joins a new group the members of the receiving network are very likely to know the cause of his leaving the old one. It will be evident from the above account that groups become subject to internal stresses and strains. Though most exhibit a good deal of stability and continuity, schisms and fissions do occur. By general consent there are legitimate reasons for switching one's allegiance. Personality clashes are an obvious one, disputes over girlfriends are another. But where there is some suggestion that a hometownsman is simply reneging on his obligations for no good reason, then secondary friendships can be used in order to clarify the circumstances. If the reasons for changing the network of allegiance appear illegitimate, the potential newcomer can be kept out. I was told by members of several Ibadan networks that this had proved effective in the sanctioning of one youth who was generally considered to have behaved badly to the closest friend who had brought him to Agege. The latter and two others had supported the new arrival and had established him in a European company after several weeks of unemployment. He then 'turned his back on his brothers' without due reason, whereupon he was excluded from other loosely-connected networks to the point at which he was forced to return to Ibadan. It was of course impossible to verify this tale. It may have been a myth, but even if it was, it nonetheless presented a salutory warning to other potential deviants.

In short, the purchase of cheap consumer goods, home-town visits, and the running of small clubs, are the main ways in which recent migrants dispose of their income surpluses. As will be evident, these are only the most modest of gains from factory employment. But there are two further points. One is that even within those networks which contain migrants employed in European firms and in which the others are at least in work, the surplus income available is generally not sufficient for network members to enjoy all these activities simultaneously. Choices have to be made between these options and selecting one denies the possibility of realizing others. Thus for example the activity which is especially valued by young men, the holding of a small ceremony with guests present, is the culmination of a period of saving in which by common consent other possible pleasures are denied. The other point is that in so far as joint saving occurs on only a limited scale, then it is easily and frequently disrupted or brought to an end. Where one (or more) member is in casual employment then money has to be set aside with a view to bribing the personnel manager of his place of employment or as a contingency to supporting him once he becomes unemployed. Since we have already indicated the nature of these difficulties they need not be repeated. What can be added is that once members of a network appear to have gained some degree of internal stability, they become especially vulnerable to being disrupted by external influences.

One of these is the home-town. Of migrants' connections with home-town relatives we have had little to say so far since in the first couple of years they expect little from absent youths. They appreciate the difficulties of becoming established in Lagos. Once they learn though that a son has gained some measure of stability, various forms of assistance become expected of him. In particular it is hoped that he will make some contribution to the school fees of his junior siblings. Of these pressures more will be said in the next chapter. For the moment it is sufficient to note that young migrants strongly resist such pressures when they are at the lower reaches of the income scale, yet when family affairs are at a crisis point, for example when a younger brother's education is at the point of being terminated, assuming some degree of responsibility is unavoidable. The individual must use up whatever slight savings he has and often enter into debt at Agege in order to make some worthwhile contribution.

The other frequent source of pressure on stable networks comes from Elders who attempt to press newly-arrived migrants on them. As we have said the norm is for migrants to arrive at Agege because they know both an Elder and a close friend in the Town. But in a minority of cases, new migrants have only an older kinsman or acquaintance of their father at Agege, and the Elder involved looks to those whom he has already helped to assume some responsibility for the newcomer. As a result, whilst network members generally choose for themselves a propitious moment at which to invite an acquaintance to join them at Agege, sometimes they have to accept a new arrival when they would prefer not do do so.[8] The request of an Elder is difficult to reject and so the intention to purchase new clothes or to go on a home-town visit has to be set aside indefinitely.

Conclusion

Most young migrants to Agege thus pass through a trying period of initiation into modern urban-industrial life. Many of the aspirations which they bring southwards to Lagos are quickly confounded and seem unlikely to be revived in the light of their early experiences. To some extent, the interpersonal relationships in which they become involved help mitigate the worst forms of hardship. Their Elders frequently prove invaluable mentors in helping them to manage difficult situations which emerge in the setting of the Town. So too with a wide circle of friendships most of which are with home-townsmen but some of which are interethnic in nature. Above all the complex set of personal relationships with urban brothers are central to an individual's continued survival in the Town and his gaining access to some form of employment on the Estate. It is these relationships, supplemented by dyadic ties with Elders and friends, which allow recent migrants to ride out the most critical periods of their early years at Agege. But the central point remains that despite the ingenuity and resourcefulness with which migrants face up to recurrent crises, the combination of low incomes and job insecurity ensures that they are for the most part primarily concerned with merely getting by within this urban industrial setting. Only at times can migrants enjoy some of the good things of urban life, and even these are modest as far as most migrants are concerned. In short, the best these young men can hope for is to oscillate irregularly between periods in which they mainly make ends meet, and brief interludes during which they have some income surplus to spend individually or collectively.

There are two final issues to be raised. The first is that in the light of the above, it is scarcely surprising that recent migrants generally voice a good deal of disenchantment with their lot whether they are employed in European companies or elsewhere. As explained in Chapter 1, the migrants have made a choice between different careers whilst they remained in their home-towns. At least in part, the decision to move southwards to the Lagos area was influenced by the apparent possibility of realizing some material gains in the short term. For most these benefits simply do not materialize, and here it should be repeated that in 1970 and 1971 inflation was running at a very high level. The possibility for gaining some material benefit thus appeared to be receding as time passed. Some migrants indeed were quite genuinely questioning whether migrating southwards was at all worthwhile. I hasten to add that they were not seriously considering returning to their home-towns. On balance, to be at Agege was preferable. But the fact that the subject was frequently raised indicates the deep disenchantment which prevailed.

Second, it must be remembered that all such attempts to deal with the instability and poverty created by wage-employment take place on the boundaries of the capital in which abound many obvious manifestations of exceptional affluence and privilege. The prosperity of the few is constantly in evidence in many superior urban locations, from the Ikeja Government Residential Area south of the factories, to Ikoyi Island in Lagos proper. Moreover, a feature which quickly becomes evident to all migrants is that personal wealth is inextricably connected with involvement in and attachment to the inner circles of government. Likewise it is evident that the resources of the State are frequently devoted to improving the conditions of those who are already rich. Of these factors we will have more to say in a later chapter. For the moment the important point to add is that the low wages of the migrants and their insecurity of employment on the expatriate-dominated Estate, are conditions which are formally sanctioned by the Nigerian government. It is such compliance by the government, coupled with their heightened sense of deprivation in the light of wider inequalities, which creates amongst the workers a generalized opposition to the wider socio-political system. To this extent, the manner in which workers organize themselves on an interpersonal basis in the Town, is for them to be also involved in a constant process of politicization.

3 Urban Careers and Self-Employment

In this chapter we turn from the social organization of recent migrants to the urban careers of more established factory workers and their efforts to become self-employed. I have already indicated that to become an independent man is a near-universal ambition amongst shopfloor workers. This ambition is most pertinently discussed with reference to the established workers, by which I refer to the minority of shopfloor employees who have been in the European firms for at least three or four years and in some instances for as many as six or seven. These men earn higher wages than the majority. Their incomes range from roughly £N18 to £N30 per month with most being towards the lower end of the scale. As will be evident from the previous chapter, these workers have passed the difficult period of simply making ends meet in the modern urban situation. They are concerned with getting on in their urban careers rather than merely getting by. This means, above all, making some headway in realizing the ambition of economic independence. In order to appreciate why becoming self-employed is so important to all shopfloor workers, it is helpful to begin from the distribution of wealth and prestige in those social contexts in which their ambitions have developed and been reinforced. These are their home-towns and Agege itself.

The Importance of Self-Employment

In urban Yorubaland generally, wealth and prestige are the preserve of self-employed men and women.[1] To begin with the distribution of wealth, at the apex of most established Yoruba towns the more affluent men are usually traders in consumer goods, transporters, contractors, builders and general store-keepers. Many of these came to local prominence in the later years of the colonial period having been previously employed by either the colonial government or expatriate trading firms. On the basis of their savings and investments from such wage-employment, often supplemented by long-service payments, they were subsequently able to set themselves up as independent businessmen. Thus the occupations of cocoa-buyer, railwaymen, civil servant, and distribution agent for trading companies, have frequently served as stepping-stones for a minority who are now prominent in their communities. In addition the more prosperous ranks include men and women who have progressed from the humble ranks of craft and trade apprentices without the advantage of either a Western education or wage-earning. In most Yoruba towns are to be found affluent businessmen who began life as bicycle-repairers, motor mechanics, blacksmiths and even labourers. Female traders almost invariably began as apprentices or petty traders in foodstuffs and cheap consumer goods, but over several decades some have become quite as wealthy as their male counterparts by virtue of hard work, judicious assessment of likely market fluctuations and sheer good fortune.

Lower down the social scale, yet above the ranks of the urban poor, there exists a stratum of self-employed men and women who, whilst engaged in relatively small-scale craft and trading enterprises, have nevertheless gained some measure of prosperity by the constant reinvestment of small profits, the taking on of apprentices and journeymen, the gradual building up of a regular clientele, and the cultivation of sound reputations for the quality of their work. These men and women reinforce the view that what wealth there is is to be realized through independent business enterprise. There are of course others, for example civil servants and older school-teachers, within long-established urban centres who have incomes equal to or greater than the more prosperous businessmen and women. But unlike the latter, these men are not positive reference points for young school-leavers such as the migrants under discussion here because their levels of formal education are considerably higher than the norm. Whilst they may be accorded elite status, strictly speaking they are not imitable figures. By contrast, many of the more affluent urban entrepreneurs have a limited degree of education or are quite illiterate. As such they can provide imitable models for younger men who have only a primary school or incomplete secondary school education.[2]

Prestige is a concomitant of wealth among urban Yoruba, and money must be used in particular ways for a more affluent person to enhance his social standing. One essential is for the wealthy man to improve the circumstances of his lineage by either making improvements to its property or by sponsoring poor or younger members. Increasingly it is expected that a man with the available finances will educate the sons of less successful siblings as well as his own male and female offspring. A further means to acquiring prestige is by the flamboyant display of wealth so that deaths, marriages and births within a wealthy man's lineage become occasions on which he engages in lavish displays which will be noted in the locality and, preferably, the town as a whole. Somewhat paradoxically, prestige is also accorded to relatively well-off men who are considered to be cautious (as opposed to miserly) in the deployment of financial assets, although the apparent paradox is easily resolved by reference to the need for a self-employed man to plan carefully for the future of his sons.

On a more general plane, the social standing of the self-employed person is always considered to be higher than that of an individual who is employed by another. Yoruba culture places a strong emphasis on sociability. The self-employed man by the very nature of his work has infinite opportunities to exercise his talents in this direction. More significant is the belief shared by all Yoruba that in order to realize his inner potential, his fate, the individual must work by himself and for himself. According to Yoruba belief, each man is born with a particular destiny which he will never know; yet only through self-help and thus self-employment will he realize it. The man who works for another is therefore considered to be passing up the opportunity of realizing his destiny in life and, in effect, demeaning himself. For these reasons too, influence and authority in established towns are predominantly the preserve of the self-employed. Having made their own way in life, they are considered best suited to helping others to do likewise. Middle-range entrepreneurs are frequently the arbiters in neighbourhood disputes, they are turned to to arrange marriages, and the urban poor approach them to use their influence to arrange apprenticeships and effect new business connections. The assets they are asked to use on behalf of others are thus consequent upon their having wide-ranging business relationships. But they are also known to be men who have made their own way in life and so, through contact with them, the urban poor hope to pick up pointers as to how they too might advance themselves.

In brief, the distribution of scarce resources in the urban settings in which they have been raised is in several respects sufficient to instil in most young men the ambition to become self-employed even before they migrate southwards. Their school-peers have frequently entered into craft and trading apprenticeships in their home-towns. They are attempting to realize some degree of social and economic mobility by entering, at the lowest levels, the entrepreneurial ladders most immediately available to them. For those who migrate, the attractions of eventually becoming self-employed at Agege are considerable; three of these are especially important.[3]

First, by virtue of the Town's size and its relative prosperity, it is able to support far more small-scale businessmen, and these exhibit a much greater variety of occupational interests than in traditional urban centres of similar size. In part this is a product of Agege having a large number of factory workers resident within its boundaries, but in the Town are substantial numbers of publically and privately-employed wage-earners who commute each day to the centre of Lagos. Whilst most Yoruba towns are expanding slowly, Agege's population increases at the rate of approximately ten per cent each year. A large proportion of this increase comprises wage-earners forced out of the suburbs of Lagos proper by the increasing cost of living within them. As a result the demand for a variety of commodities and services is continually increasing. Not only does the demand for new housing provide work for builders, contractors, traders in cement and roofing materials and electricians, but the increasing number of wage-earning residents is served by a myriad of small-scale businessmen satisfying a wide variety of needs. So, within the Town there are numerous economic niches to be filled and an increasing variety of specialist skills is required. Moreover, many of these do not require the extended apprenticeships of three to five years which those entering into trade and craftsmanship in established towns must undertake. For the most part men can move in and out of these entrepreneurial realms at will.

Second, the economic returns from self-employment in Agege are considerably higher than elsewhere. This is most especially the case amongst the Town's Big Men and its more successful female traders. In the more capital-intensive enterprises such as contracting, transporting and bulk trading, individuals frequently earn several thousand pounds per annum, in some cases more than £N10,000. These are wealthy urban residents by any standards and they own either several-storey tenement buildings or smart lavishly furnished modern bungalows. Big Men can indulge in other forms of conspicuous consumption, such as the holding of expensive ceremonies, whilst also educating their children and contributing to the improvement of their family property. At the same time the Town has a substantial stratum of middle-range self-employed men and women amongst whom annual incomes of between £N500 and £N2,000 are relatively common. These well to do entrepreneurs comprise an occupationally diverse social category: amongst them one finds carpenters, builders, butchers, produce-buyers, motor mechanics and traders in a wide range of commodities. Their shared characteristic however is that they are the individual owners of the Town's tenement buildings. In their chosen entrepreneurial spheres, they have had periods of noteworthy business success, and they have used their profits to construct the eight or ten room buildings which are the most common form of housing in the Town. Subsequently, using the rents from wage-earners and self-employed tenants, they have built up and diversified their businesses further. For such men and women, urban life is secure and relatively comfortable. They own a moderate range of more expensive consumer goods — bicycles, radios, refrigerators, and electrical equipment — they are able to educate their sons through secondary school, and they are able to dress well. The longer term intention of the Town's well to do is to retire to their home-towns. With this end in mind some have constructed new homes there, or contributed financially to the renewal of existing buildings. The circumstances of the Big Men and the well to do thus indicate that there is greater prosperity available at Agege than in urban settlements of comparable size elsewhere in Yorubaland.

Third, Agege is essentially an open community in that there are opportunities for individual socio-economic mobility. Not only are there many rewarding entrepreneurial niches in the Town, but there are also opportunities for those with limited amounts of capital to enter and expand these niches through hard work, steady reinvestment, and good judgement. This has been the pattern over the past twenty years, and it is reflected in the careers of the currently prosperous. The majority of Big Men and well to do entrepreneur-landlords, most of whom are now in middle age, initially came to Agege as craft apprentices and traders of limited means. Typically their early years were ones of poverty as bicycle-repairers, tailors, apprentice motor mechanics and carpenters. Yet from the early 1950s when the population began to rise considerably, many of them were able to expand their businesses into ones of substance.

It is significant that the business enterprises of such men are highly personalized. Also important is that they face the common problem of increasing marginal costs in the supervision of employees to the point at which they are not able to do their own work effectively. For these reasons they are unable to continually take up the ever-rising demand for goods and services. The opportunities to do so remain open to the self-employed of lesser means. The result is that in the Town's economically and socially heterogeneous neighbourhoods one finds not only Big Men and entrepreneur-landlords who have benefitted in the past from urban expansion: they also include a minority of self-employed men and women who are now likewise taking up opportunities and are, despite their humble origins, manifestly rising up the socio-economic scale. Thus for example in the locality in which I resided there were several noteworthy 'spiralists'[4]: a thirty-three year old man, previously an apprentice motor mechanic, who had been able to purchase a second-hand passenger bus, an electrician in his early twenties who after being journeyman to a builder was engaged in the wiring of new tenement buildings, and a young woman beginning as a cloth trader after several years of minor trading activity. All these people were moving into the more lucrative realms of urban entrepreneurship and so their mobility was all the more noteworthy. To these might be added others whose degree of social and economic improvement was less striking yet were nevertheless effecting some individual advancement in the Town's expanding economy.

I have presented here only sketches of socio-economic differentiation in those urban contexts with which the migrants are most familiar. Much of the above is a considerable over-simplification,[5] but I hope it makes clear why it is that young migrants are excessively concerned with saving from wage-employment in order to become independent men. Before migrating, the distribution of wealth and prestige in their home-town locales has shown that the key to individual advancement lies in self-employment. By comparison farming, the occupation of most of their fathers, holds out no prospects at all. Within Agege itself it is amongst the self-employed that the bulk of available wealth is distributed, and the backgrounds of those with wealth, as well as the experiences of those currently in the process of rising up the social scale, indicate to the migrants that they too can share in this prosperity provided that they can acquire the necessary capital to enter into the entrepreneurial system in the first instance. It is this substantial obstacle which they must overcome.

One point which requires emphasis is that in Agege as in the towns of Yorubaland generally, there are no forms of wage-employment, whether under private employers or the State, which are open to the migrants and which match the prospects for mobility afforded by self-employment. Of course many wage-earning posts in Lagos are highly paid but, because most migrants have a relatively low level of formal schooling, they are automatically excluded from them. In the factories, as we shall see in later chapters, the prospects for most workers of gaining any marked improvement on an individual or a collective basis are slight indeed. It will be pointed out in the next chapter that there are exceedingly few opportunities for shop-floor men to rise up into white-collar or supervisory posts on the Estate. In Chapter 5 it will be shown that even where house unions operate to some effect, nevertheless the general wage increases realized scarcely keep their incomes in step with current levels of inflation. In other words, for a migrant to anticipate a life-time career in factory work is to resign himself to a highly restricted life-style and an equally restricted range of life-chances for his children. On the other hand, whilst the incomes of many self-employed men and women are low, but not lower than those of factory workers, at least self-employment allows the opportunity of socio-economic mobility in the longer run. It is this opportunity to advance themselves which the migrants seek.

For reasons which will become evident, however, it is worth stressing that it is not only a matter of seeking higher material rewards. Although primarily that, it is also a question of status and self-esteem. Low incomes apart, by common consent wage-employment in any form condemns the individual to a perpetually low social rank. Agege people recognize that for young migrants to become factory workers is an unavoidable starting point to their working lives, and for the migrants themselves their immediate low status is of little consequence. There is, though, a minority of middle-aged men in the Town who are engaged in wage-employment, not on the Estate as factory workers, but as employees of the State or smaller private companies in the Lagos metropolitan area. Both the economic and the social standing of these men serve as a severe reminder to the young migrants as to their later circumstances in life if they do not escape from wage-employment into self-employment. The majority of these men, who have their wives and children at Agege, must rent urban accommodation and they have only a limited range of personal

Urban Careers and Self-Employment

possessions. In economic terms, their standard of living is simply not comparable with that of well to do entrepreneurs, and their social rank in the Town is of the lowest order. They are considered, through lack of ambition, to have passed up any opportunity of getting on in life. They are also believed to have abrogated their responsibilities to their families, in particular to their sons. Thus it is frequently asked of such men: 'How can a man help his sons to get on in life when he has not been able to help himself?'. Young factory workers share in this low opinion. They often sanction and ridicule their middle-aged counterparts whilst in the same breath expressing a firm determination not to share their fate.

Careers and Conflicts

It will be evident from Chapter 2 that for recent migrants the aspiration to become economically independent is not yet of real consequence for how they organize their social relations. For established workers the situation is different. Since they are the more long-standing employees of the European firms, they have benefited from annual increments and the general wage increases gained through union action. Their wages are by no means substantial, but they are in excess of the level needed to meet their basic requirements, and as such these workers can turn their attention to saving with a view to self-employment. Indeed some have actually attempted to effect the status passage into urban entrepreneurship in Agege. These are a minority of workers, for only a few of those employed in European companies have had the opportunity to save and to move into self-employment. For example, my own neighbourhood contained some 100 factory workers and over one hundred and thirty self-employed males. Only eight of the latter were previously factory workers on the Estate. (Most of the remainder were middle-aged men who had long been self-employed or younger men who, after being apprenticed, were now self-employed without any interim experience of wage-earning.) This being so, to make generalizations is difficult particularly in relation to the workers-turned-entrepreneurs. But this does not, I believe, seriously detract from the points I wish to establish below, the most important of these being that the obstacles to becoming self-employed are considerable, if not insuperable.

While all migrants with due pragmatism acknowledge the barriers to their becoming independent men, they also have a fairly clear idea as to how their urban careers need to progress in order to realize their ambitions. They share a kind of cognitive career chart which points up how ideally they might order their lives and their interpersonal relationships to best effect. The first necessary stage is for them to organize their interpersonal relationships in Agege in order to maximize on their savings capacities. The second stage (although it must run parallel with the first) is for them to organize their relationships with those in their places of origin to the same end. The third requirement is that they must make a realistic assessment of the finances necessary not only to buy equipment and rent a shop or store, but also to sustain themselves during the initial few months of self-employment whilst a range of customers is established. Finally the workers hope to make a rational and calculated entry into their chosen field of employment. This stage is obviously best effected at a point where they have the best possibility of survival and a good chance for subsequently capitalizing on the opportunities available for further advancement. Above all, this means that they need quite substantial capital sums in hand. Note this is no more than an ideal model as to how they might proceed. It provides the workers with a rudimentary map as to the essential steps required if they are to realize their longer term ambitions, and workers well realize that departures will have to be made from this ideal. We can also use this career map as an analytic aid in order to illustrate systematically the major obstacles which face established workers. It is possible in other words to use their construction in an heuristic fashion. Let us look first at the problems arising from the nature of their interpersonal relationships in the context of the Town.

It has been pointed out that migrants' social networks generally include employees of both European and non-European firms, and that within these there exists a high degree of trust and reciprocity. These considerations present difficulties for established workers since they must change the nature of their friendships in order to begin to save. The situation which commonly emerges is that one or two members of a network employed in European firms move away from the minimum wage-level and anticipate further wage increases in the future. By contrast, other network members remain employed in non-European firms near to the minimum wage-level whilst the most recent are still in casual employment. The result is that those in European firms are continually subsidizing their less fortunate fellows rather than beginning to save from their higher incomes. Hence, interpersonal relationships with urban brothers have to be redefined and, in some instances, set aside altogether. The problem is that not only has it frequently been a matter of sheer chance that one network member rather than the others has gained the preferable type of employment, but more often than not, he has gained it by virtue of the support provided by his less fortunate urban brothers.

One Ijebu worker whom I knew found himself in precisely this position. He was earning a little over £N17 per month whilst the highest income amongst the remaining three members of his network was £N13. He was the only member to be employed in a European firm but it was through the financial support of his fellows that he had gained this employment after arriving in the Town. The extent of reciprocity was now operating greatly to his personal disadvantage and he found it difficult to set aside more than a couple of pounds each month. But, as he commented to me: 'What can I do in these circumstances? These men are my brothers and we have shared all. In order to save, can I now turn away from them?' This plaintive remark was prompted by another member of the network having recently brought his younger brother to Agege, and the costs of supporting him were substantially falling on the best-off member of the network. It is this kind of situation which frequently emerges and which proves especially galling. The better-paid member (or members) of a network begins to save on a small scale only to have the regular pattern which he must establish, severely disrupted by another's difficult circumstances.

The general response is for established workers to partly mitigate the retrograde influence of others by increasingly privatizing their relationships. This is one of the further reasons why networks of home-townsmen change their composition over time. The better-paid members of the same network, or of different networks, break away and establish themselves as a relatively independent social unit in order to establish a pattern of concentrated saving. It is not presented in this light. Instead some other form of explanation is found in order to make the break an apparently legitimate one, and effect it without rancour. Thus in the case of the Ijebu worker to whom I have referred, some two months after the new migrant's arrival, he moved in with an Egba factory worker who had long been his close friend and was slightly better paid than himself on the grounds that the tenement room was now overcrowded and uncomfortable. This does not necessarily lead to an end in the demands made by the less fortunate others, but it does allow of some restriction on the regularity with which these are made. Being physically separate means that others are less likely to know the established worker's immediate state of affairs, and it becomes possible to find excuses for setting aside continued requests for financial support.

Only on rare occasions though can better-paid workers entirely set aside all obligations to others. For the most part the sense of responsibility to others is too substantial to be cast off completely. Still less are established workers prepared to run the gamut of being labelled as misers and self-centred individuals who have completely set aside their responsibilities to their urban brothers. It is on this count that the first departure occurs from the ideal situation which workers envisage. Rather than completely redefining interpersonal relationships with significant others in the Town, they attempt to effect some form of compromise between self-interest and a sense of obligation to those who find themselves in dire straits. This however is of rather less importance than the compromises which established workers have to make between pursuing their own intentions to save and acknowledging the interests of relatives in their places of origin.

In broad terms, the demands emanating from the home-town increase in proportion to the evident security and relative prosperity of the established worker and, once acknowledged, they cut heavily into his ability to save. During the migrants' first two or three years at Agege, little more is expected of them but occasional home-town visits and, at such times, the distribution of a small range of gifts costing no more than a couple of pounds. After three years or so the situation often becomes radically transformed.

Increasingly there are indications that migrants' parents expect financial assistance from their absent sons. At least initially these Yoruba migrants respond in a somewhat contrasting fashion to the apparent norm amongst migrants elsewhere in urban Africa. The general pattern appears for migrants to be eager and anxious to assume many responsibilities to those in their places of origin.[6] By contrast the migrants to Agege enter into a wide range of delaying tactics and subterfuges. They try to hide their improved circumstances from home-town people. Workers omit from their letters the fact that they have found permanent employment. They fail to mention the wage increases which they have received. On the occasion of home-town visits they play down the improvements they have realized, whilst painting the most dismal image possible of Lagos life. Some subterfuges become quite elaborate and are all the more embarrassing when they are revealed. One migrant from Ibadan, for example, by his fifth year at Agege was securely employed in a European company and was earning some £N19.10s. per month after having gained a couple of special promotions, yet in his communications with his father and on home-town visits he made no mention of these improvements in his circumstances, 'because if he hears of this then he will bring pressure that I should marry'. He was able to get away with this for some time since on their visits to Ibadan, his Agege brothers maintained the same fiction when they visited his father. Eventually the tactic broke down when a fellow migrant worker, not acquainted with the situation on hand, happened to let out to the father that his son was doing relatively well. This was followed by a considerable dispute which took several weeks to cool off.

This worker, as with all established workers, was thus faced with the critical issue as to how much influence the wishes and expectations of home-town relatives should have in the development of his own career. For most this is an acute problem. While in the context of Agege the migrant factory workers are underprivileged, in the context of the home-town setting they are seen as privileged young men by virtue of their having received some education. Even if a young man has received only a primary schooling, nevertheless he is better off than the majority of uneducated people at home. Moreover the material costs, as well as the opportunity cost, to his parents will have drained some of their limited resources from farming or urban craft employment. Far more demanding has been the expense of any degree of secondary school education. A single term's fees range from between £N25 to £N30 which means that parents and other close relatives have had to make considerable sacrifices in order to keep a youth in school for two or three years. Especially relevant apropos these expectations is that a large proportion of migrants are the first or second sons of their fathers and so the latter, who are generally polygamous, are looking to them with a keen eye for assistance in meeting the costs of younger sons' secondary education. These expectations are quite at odds with established workers' attempts to save.

In the resulting disputes some kind of compromise has to be reached, and delaying tactics and subterfuges notwithstanding, the result is invariably to the disadvantage of the workers. There are three recurrent issues. The overriding one is simply the amount of money which a worker is to contribute to a younger sibling's education. Since he has (at least as viewed from a considerable distance) a regular income which allows him a degree of prosperity in excess of most family members, then he is often pressed into giving a particular sum as a firm commitment. Workers try to avoid such a situation wherever possible but on the whole have little success in doing so.

Urban Careers and Self-Employment

The most common commitment appears to be between £N20 and £N30 per annum, roughly one term's fees. The second concerns the location in which a sibling's secondary education is to occur; for parents are often of the opinion that the standard of schooling in Lagos is of a higher standard than in their home-towns. Since established workers are frequently in their late twenties and therefore mature enough to care for a younger brother, they are pressed into assuming full responsibility for a junior sibling's welfare and training at Agege. Again workers usually resist such pressures, not so much because of the expenses incurred on a day to day basis but because, should there be a short-fall of available school-fees, then the pressure is entirely on them to make it up, most likely by drawing on their own savings. It does however happen that established workers capitulate under such pressure, in particular where they are from villages distant from the larger towns where secondary schools are generally concentrated. The third issue for dispute between migrants and parents is to how many junior siblings are to be supported. Having assisted in the education of one sibling for two or three years, then it is expected that a worker will continue such assistance for the next junior brother in line. Conflicts over such expectations are somewhat infrequent because of the relatively short length of time most workers have been in wage-employment. Most workers I knew said they intended to support one sibling and then draw the line, but it is difficult to imagine this occurring considering its implications, and I never encountered an established worker who had actually done this. For most workers the responsibility to assist in the payment of school fees is one which has to be continued and this constitutes a substantial drain on already slender savings capacities.

The above account is based on conversations with established workers. I was not able to observe such negotiations and conflicts between themselves and their parents in the contexts of their home-towns. On at least two occasions migrants to whom I was particularly close took me along on their home-town visits because it was felt that my presence would avoid as yet latent tensions coming to the surface! A somewhat unusual and striking illustration of these processes involved an Egba worker whose mother was also resident at Agege and owned the tenement building in which he lived rent free with most of his needs provided for. In 1968 and 1969 this had allowed Aminu to make contributions totalling roughly £N30 each year to the school fees of his mother's brother's daughter. In 1970, his fifth year of wage-earning, his circumstances changed. His wage rose to £N18.15s. per month and he determined to make a great effort to save with a view to becoming an electrician in the Town. This was clearly incompatible with keeping up the school fee contributions. His mother had been instrumental in initiating the arrangement and so Aminu broached the issue with her and the girl's father, suggesting that since the girl's performance was abysmal, she would be better off as a trading apprentice. His mother dismissed the suggestion outright: the girl's limited ability made her continuing at school all the more imperative. Faced with this firm stance, Aminu paid £N10 as a contribution to the first term's fees.

By the second term he was quite resolved to draw the line and refused outright to make a contribution. The confrontation with his mother was extreme. She accused him of selfishness, ingratitude, and a lack of concern for others' well-being. After a fortnight of dispute which culminated in Aminu threatening to leave his mother's house, he found an unexpected ally in the girl's father who had also decided the money was being wasted. Her education was abruptly terminated. There were several rather exceptional considerations here, and Aminu was especially successful in negotiating his existing obligations in relation to his ambitions. This brief account, however, does indicate the problems which it involves. Established workers attempting to pursue a regular pattern of savings are open to heavy sanctioning and, as in this instance, accusations of outright selfishness. Any migrant would prefer to avoid such a situation wherever possible, quite apart from their genuine concern for the education of their junior siblings. The moral dilemma is insoluble and some balance of interests has to be found. Whatever form this takes, it nevertheless sets back a concerted effort to save.

The support of junior relatives in school is only one recurrent bone of contention with parents at home. The other major issue is the question of marriage. Since established workers are older than most migrants, as time passes their parents become the more insistent that their sons should marry. According to the workers themselves this is because parents fear that they will enter into a 'Lagos marriage', a temporary union which can be easily broken off by either partner, or that they will marry a 'Lagos girl' which for many has connotations of prostitution. It is though, the question of timing rather than the prospect of marriage as such which is the subject of dispute, for it is also at this later stage of their urban careers that they seriously contemplate it as a possibility.

To marry a girl from their place of origin is the ideal for most migrants. Most do not contemplate the possibility of marrying a girl who does not come from the same town or Yoruba kingdom as themselves. There are many reasons for this but in major part it is because migrants have particular qualities in mind for their potential spouses: to select one from their home-towns allows them the widest possible choice. They generally feel that their wives should have a primary education, they should be domestically adept, preferably they will be physically attractive. Their wives should have also some entrepreneurial expertise in their own right. This factor plays a significant part in the choice of wives. In addition to acquiring domestic skills many Yoruba girls enter into apprenticeships in their early 'teens either under their mothers or other self-employed women. Established workers feel that if they can select wives with apprenticeships behind them, then these talents can be used to advance their own entrepreneurial ambitions. In Agege there are many spheres of entrepreneurship which are dominated by women: hairdressing, sewing, and petty trade are the largest ones, but there are others. If a wife is able to gain a preliminary foothold in one such economic niche, her husband can then invest his own savings in her enterprise. Thus she contributes to the household budget in her own right, and her income can be used to tide her husband over the difficult period of changing from wage-employment to self-employment when it is expected that his economic return will be low. For these reasons, when making their home-town visits, migrants draw on all available resources to find a wife with proven entrepreneurial skills. They can draw on the knowledge of urban brothers and information from mothers and sisters can be utilized to this end. In some cases it can produce notable dividends. For example an established worker from Otta, the capital of Aworiland to the immediate north of Agege, chose his wife primarily (according to his account) on the basis that she had already demonstrated considerable expertise in trading in foodstuffs. When he brought her to Agege, he gave her some £N30 from his savings. This she, along with two young apprentices, used to purchase commodities from Otta Market where she had many connections for resale at Agege Market where foodstuff prices are considerably higher. Her monthly income after a year at Agege was in the region of £N8 and the couple's cost of living was relatively low since, after rent, food is the major recurrent expenditure of all Town residents. The husband estimated that he was now able to save almost £N10 per month from his wage whereas before marriage it was only a matter of two or three pounds.

On the other hand marriage, more often than not, seriously depletes established workers' existing funds of capital and sets back their attempts to save regularly. The process of selecting a wife from the home-town is frequently a lengthy process requiring several visits. Courtship is itself costly since Yoruba girls expect gifts to indicate that a suitor usually absent from the town is serious in his intentions; and a returning migrant has to be somewhat generous to his prospective parents-in-law for the same reason.[7] The major expenditures occur when workers bring their wives to Agege, for there can be no question of a wife remaining in her parental home once married. In order to ensure some degree of privacy, the worker must move away from those urban brothers with whom he has previously shared cheap accommodation: the cost of a single tenement room now falls entirely on himself and this he must furnish to provide his wife with some comfort. The recurrent outlay on food similarly increases. Finally while workers make attempts to establish their newly-arrived spouses in some entrepreneurial capacity in Agege, although the initial outlay may be considerable (as with the purchase of a sewing machine for example), the return is usually only a couple of pounds per month since all female-dominated occupations are highly competitive and allow a relatively meagre return. Indeed many such endeavours fade away quite quickly, not least because wives are frequently pregnant before marriage or become so soon after.

To recap, whilst the workers' ideal course of career progesss contains, as it must, a strong emphasis on the continuous renegotiation of their interpersonal relationships at Agege and *vis-à-vis* their home-towns, they have little choice but to make considerable departures from the ideal. To be able to maximize their savings, established wage-earners would have to reject the urban brothers with whom they have spent their early years in the Town, to set themselves firmly against the further education of their younger siblings, and in doing so to declare a lack of a sense of obligation and duty to their parents. Finally they would have to greatly delay their marriages. A few workers who are utterly committed to realizing their economic independence come quite near to the ideal course of saving and self-advancement. But in doing so they come in for a great deal of personal criticism. They are often disliked and condemned as 'self-seekers'. The extent of saving which their incomes allow is nevertheless limited. One worker in my own neighbourhood consistently refused to recognize any outstanding debts to his urban brothers in the Town, cut off virtually all association with his family at Ijebu Ode, and intended, at thirty one, to delay marriage for as long as possible. From his earnings of £N26 per month his savings amounted to only £N10. Another migrant, from Ibadan, and, like the Ijebu, living alone in the Town, only rarely visited his home-town, had no financial responsibilities there, and was unmarried. Yet out of £N29 per month his savings totalled only about £N13 to £N14.

Now it will be remembered that on arrival at Agege the migrants, whilst ambitious to become independent men, have little idea as to how much they require in the way of savings or as to how long they will remain in wage employment. In time, however, they develop a rough and ready, but realistic, idea as to the starting capital required to establish a business at a level which will allow a reasonable prospect for continued survival. It varies according to the particular sphere of entrepreneurship. But it seems agreed, and self-employed men tend to support this consensus, that at least £N200 to £N300 is required to enter such occupations as trader, motor mechanic, electrician, and builder, whilst half as much again is required to become a contractor, a trader in cloth or building materials, or the owner of a small shop. Thus if one assumes, as I think it is reasonable to do, that established workers are at best able to save about £N50 a year, then their period of saving is going to be a lengthy one. It will last perhaps five to ten years, in addition to the early years spent in irregular and low paid employment. According to a survey which I conducted in one factory,[8] these seem to be the lengths of time which shopfloor workers themselves have in mind. All other things being equal, established workers face lengthy further periods in the factories. But the point to be particularly noted is that it is most unlikely that 'other things' will remain equal, and most developments will raise further obstacles to workers' realizing their ambitions. For a start as they become older, so their home-town obligations are likely to become more substantial and pressing. As their fathers age or die, so first or second sons will face further pressures to assist their families financially. Then again, as established workers become older, the costs of keeping their own families in Agege will increase. In a few years their own children will be going to primary school and within a decade will be at the point of entering secondary school. Finally, and most important of all, the costs of entry into virtually all spheres of urban entrepreneurship are rising, and at a rate greater than wage increases in the Ikeja factories. We will return to these considerations later. But they are important to introduce here for two reasons. First, in so far as established workers generally concede these problems, so they compound their sense of being faced with massive obstacles to their urban career prospects. Second, they also help to explain why the majority of workers currently attempting to move into self-employment do so in a precipitate fashion despite the commonly appreciated hazards which this involves. To these men we now turn.

From Factory Work to Self-Employment

Here again, the circumstances of the workers involved are considerably at odds with the ideal career pattern outlined earlier. The major departures are three-fold.

The first is that becoming self-employed is more a precipitate action than a carefully calculated act. It is usually triggered by one or two particular fortuitous circumstances rather than workers having achieved the combination of assets which they consider ideally necessary for establishing their enterprises. This is not to say, as we shall see, that there is no degree of calculation in their attempting to move from the factories into self-employment. In no sense are attempts at making the transition irrational. But the move has not been preceded by the methodical build-up of capital, access to a store or shop, and the development of a range of useful contacts, which both factory workers and self-employed men consider necessary for entrepreneurial success. The second point of departure is that it is effected with capital sums in hand considerably lower than most would consider ideal. As indicated above, it is agreed that some £N200 to £N300 is necessary for enterprises to not merely survive in this highly competitive entrepreneurial milieu but also to manifest some degree of growth over time. Established workers well know that the overall profitability of any independent business enterprise is in substantial part a function of the initial capital outlay. Therefore if they are to have any chance of becoming relatively successful men in the longer run, (on the lines of for example the middle-aged entrepreneur-landlords of the present day), then they need to enter their respective economic niches at a reasonably high level of capital investment. In fact those who attempt to become self-employed do so with minimal amounts of capital in hand. And this results, the third consideration, in many instances of outright failure with a briefly independent man having to return to wage-employment with his earlier savings expended.

In that we are discussing here only a very small minority of shop-floor workers, it is inappropriate to talk of typical examples. A further methodological and presentational problem is that one has to rely heavily on the interpretations which those involved place on their own past experiences. However, two case-studies will help to substantiate these generalizations.

1. The Case of the Failed Electrician

For some men in the Town, being an electrician is a lucrative occupation. It is also a prestigious one since it is a specifically modern craft role, it allows extensive social contact with men of wealth and standing, and electricians can build up their enterprises by taking on a handful of young apprentices. Adamson, as with most workers who aspire to this role, estimated that with about £N200, an ex-factory worker who knew his job could become fairly well off over time. On arrival from Ibadan in 1963, he was fortunate in gaining employment in an Ikeja paint-producing factory, a European firm in which he quickly became a permanent employee. He had already picked up a rudimentary training in electrical repair work at Ibadan and for a time pursued a correspondence course, although he abandoned this when in 1968 he married an Ibadan girl. By this time he was earning £N19 per month which he supplemented by occasional moonlighting under an established electrician living in his neighbourhood. This experience convinced him, he said, that he could not stay in factory work 'because with my education (a completed primary-schooling) there was no promotion in the factory'. For the next two years he and his wife tried all means of saving. Although, as he put it, 'I was held back by my relatives, their demands were too great', he managed to scrape together £N65. At this point his father died and from the elder brother who inherited his father's Ibadan clothing store, Adamson claimed a further £N50. This meant that his capital in hand was considerably less than he had anticipated. He nevertheless decided that this was the moment at which he should try to become an independent man against a background of blocked promotion in the factory. In other words, the inheritance triggered off a somewhat precipitate decision, and with help from a relative, a trained carpenter, he rented a small shop and converted it into a workplace.

His first job proved disastrous. Having been contracted to wire a trader's new house, he drew on some of his limited capital. When the job was finished, the trader accused him of overpricing and poor workmanship. He paid Adamson only half the price agreed for the job and all attempts to recover the loss proved to no avail. During the next five weeks several small jobs showed only marginal profit and within two months he was desperately short of money, to the point at which he had to find casual work. He then managed to gain a further contract to rewire an old house and from this he made a profit of some £N15. Subsequently however, no further work was forthcoming. After three months in another casual post he had the chance of becoming a permanent worker in a new textile firm, but in order to secure the post by paying the necessary bribe, he had to sell off his equipment. With this, his attempt at economic independence was at an end.

The disastrous initial encounter with the trader indicates the need for workers entering self-employment to have more capital in hand than that simply required for a shop, basic equipment and raw materials. Any self-employed person at Agege expects to encounter something similar to Adamson's experiences. With his non-existent reputation and lack of business contacts, Adamson had little chance of recovering his feet without substantial savings to tide him over the preliminary period of economic independence. Thus in certain respects Adamson's move appears somewhat foolhardy and is clearly at odds with the ideal course of making the transition. On the other hand, and this is an important point, as far as Adamson could foresee he was unlikely to be in a more propitious circumstance for making the leap into the realm of entrepreneurship. He was finding the process of saving extremely slow and home-town ties were proving a stumbling block to the maximization of his savings capacity. His wage was unlikely to rise much in the next few years whilst the costs of becoming an electrician were rising all the time due to general inflation. So, as Adamson put it:

'The inheritance I thought was a god-send. For when in the future was I likely to have £N100 in my pocket. I thought to myself: "As a factory worker it may never be the case for life is hard" — and so I went ahead'.

This in broad terms is the rationale expounded by those who have attempted self-employment and failed. Faced with a particularly fortuitous circumstance or set of events, they have adopted a 'now-or-never' approach. To this extent, their attempts have some degree of rationality underpinning them: whilst they have an ideal model of how their circumstances should be ordered, they are also quite pragmatic about their dismal prospects for the future.

2. The Case of the Successful Motor Mechanic

Akin, a migrant from Ijebu Ode, was amongst the first cadre of wage-earners in an Ikeja tyre-producing firm. This he considered was an appropriate workplace since he intended to become a motor mechanic. Subsequently he married Taiwo a trained seamstress also from Ijebu, and purchased for her a second-hand sewing machine. By late 1968 his wage stood at £N24 per month and, with his wife's assistance, he was able to save and contribute slightly to a junior brother's school fees. In the same year he began to work at weekends for a local motor mechanic and, as with Adamson's moonlighting, this experience encouraged him to seriously consider making the leap into self-employment.

By early 1970, he had accumulated a little over £N100 from his wages and added to it a further £N15, his Christmas bonus payment from the factory. This fell considerably short of the £N250 which he had in mind as his capital savings target. Two particular factors precipitated his attempt in that year to leave wage-employment. One was that his application for training as a section head was refused for the third time and for the same reason as previously, his incomplete secondary education. The other was that the man for whom he occasionally moonlighted was forced to leave Agege. Akin was thus presented with the opportunity of renting the vacant lot and perhaps

Urban Careers and Self-Employment

assuming the somewhat slight trade that went with it. The other considerations which influenced his decision were that Taiwo was having some degree of success as a seamstress (he estimated her monthly income at around £N6), and he was able to borrow some £N20 from his father's brother who, when he visited home, had encouraged him to rent the vacant repair yard. In all Akin had £N135 in hand when he resigned from the factory.

For the first six months business was exceptionally slow. Akin had two apprentices but there was little to occupy them. He spent the greater part of his time attempting to drum up trade from bus and lorry owners in the Town. Such jobs as did come his way involved repairing well-pump machinery, food-grinding equipment, a local printer's machinery and so on. Throughout this period as he commented, 'We were living a hand to mouth existence', and here Taiwo's small income proved invaluable. Yet by the middle of 1971, business had begun to pick up somewhat, for several lorry and bus owners were coming to him, a good sign since such work is the mainstay of Agege mechanics generally. Nevertheless his income was low, for the most part he estimated between £N10 and £N15 per month.

As with the description of Adamson's career, this is a much abbreviated account. Clearly though, several particular factors played a major part in influencing Akin's decision to set wage-employment behind him. Firstly, a wage bonus could be added to his limited savings. Second, more by chance than design, he received a small loan from a wealthier kinsman. But as Akin himself emphasized, his decision was precipitated by his being rejected for promotion within the factory and the availability of the small mechanic's yard. Akin had been in the same firm for some seven years in all. He had had no exceptional promotions, only a steady and slight progression up the wages scale as is customary for shopfloor workers. Being turned down for the third time for training as a section head heightened the limited prospects which he faced for as long as he remained a wage-earner. Finally, whilst for some months previously it had seemed likely that the mechanic with whom he occasionally worked would have to leave the Town, the fact that he did so shortly after

Akin was rejected for promotion seems to have been especially crucial.

Here then was a very particular combination of circumstances, the nature of which was scarce likely to be repeated. Subsequently, whilst Akin's monthly income was well below his previous wage, nevertheless the enterprise was reasonably secure. In Akin's own words:

> 'At least I am now an independent man and can hold my head high. Before I was as a slave at the mercy of all managers. Now I am my own master. My wife and my sons later on will be proud of me. That is all that matters'.

In his case the considerable risk he had taken and the subsequent hardship had proved well worthwhile.

The Restrictions on Self-Advancement

So we have here two contrasting experiences, one of failure, the other of success. Both equally demonstrate that it is particular circumstances and particular events which push forward the workers into urban entrepreneurship. Far from having carefully prepared the ground for the passage from wage-employment into self-employment, workers respond precipitately to situations which appear to allow them some opportunity, however slight, of gaining a foothold in the entrepreneurial sector. The crucial point to be added to these is that whilst, as acknowledged earlier, these cannot be taken as typical examples, the experiences of the few workers who attempt self-employment are in general much more on the lines of Adamson's failure than Akin's success. That is to say, the norm is for aspirant entrepreneurs to run into great difficulties on entering into their chosen economic spheres. The small amounts of capital which they have in hand plus the extreme competitiveness of small-scale entrepreneurship are such as to ensure that they teeter on the brink of failure for varying periods of time. And they are, on the whole, forced back into wage-employment once again. This is almost invariably the case with workers who have become tailors, for example. This is an occupation which is especially attractive to those most eager to escape from factory work. It can be taken up with as little as £N50 to £N60 in hand, for all that is required is a second-hand sewing machine, a few pieces of fabric, and a small workshop. On the other hand tailoring is an intensely competitive sphere of self-employment and those involved must operate at the lowest possible profit margins. Most do not last for more than a few months before they can no longer make ends meet and must revert to factory employment.

The same is to be said, however, of most who chance their arm in the entrepreneurial sphere: and to this extent their attempts appear somewhat foolhardy. At the same time it must be emphasized that the 'now or never' approach contains its calculated element. Whilst the transition is triggered by particular considerations rather than ideal circumstances, the individuals involved do weigh up most carefully the options available to them. In acknowledging the difficulties which they will most likely face in the future, so they estimate this to be the best possible course of action open to them. They recognize that home-town pressures are likely to increase rather than decline, that the costs of bringing up their own families at Agege will also increase, and that the costs of entry into entrepreneurship are constantly rising due to general inflation. It is scarcely surprising that those who have the opportunity adopt a 'now or never' approach. The chance may never emerge again: they have at least the possibility of gaining a foothold, and even if they do not progress far within the entrepreneurial realm, they can enjoy the prestige and personal satisfaction of being self-employed as opposed to enduring in resigned fashion the low status of the factory employee.

In relation to the present analysis however, the more important concerns are the ramifications of this unfolding situation for the majority of shopfloor workers who are well aware that most such attempts fail and that only a few have a modicum of success. The efforts of such men as Adamson and Akin take place in full view of other factory workers. They continue to reside in the same neighbourhoods as their ex-colleagues and some depend heavily on the latter for much of their business. Because of the great relevance of their experiences to others, their efforts raise considerable interest and much local comment. It might be added that such comment contains a notably ambivalent thread, for on the one hand, workers often express some degree of admiration for the boldness of those who as it were have the courage of their convictions. They are felt to be demonstrating precisely the risk-taking qualities which are essential for successful urban entrepreneurship. On the other hand, they are also considered excessively optimistic. It is clear from the way in which most function that their enterprises are going to be run on a shoe-string, and this is in a competitive milieu in which everyone well knows that weak enterprises with limited assets go quickly to the wall. Their likely failure is frequently anticipated. It becomes a matter for public discussion not so much as to whether they will fail but as to how long they will last.

The crucial point here is that, in the light of the experiences of this minority, the majority of workers are made fully aware of the tremendous obstacles which they face in the future, and of the absolute necessity of postponing any attempt to move into self-employment until they possess the maximum possible amount of capital savings. Yet as all are equally aware, this process is in itself problematic in the extreme. The results are to produce a generalized sense of despair as to their future circumstances and the workers' sense of hostility to conditions of employment on the Estate is considerably heightened since they see that the root of their problem lies in the low wage-levels which are the starting point for all efforts to realize their longer-term ambitions. As the workers themselves interpret the situation, it appears they are increasingly trapped by a productive system and reward structure which is quite at odds with the ambitions which brought them to the Lagos metropolitan area.

While this despondency is prevalent it is not, at least as yet, sufficient to result in workers' abandoning their aspirations to become self-employed. No doubt it will do so in the future, for the most probable longer term development within the Ikeja area is that most workers will remain where they are today. It seems highly unlikely that within the space of the next five or ten years there will be a gradual out-flow of workers from the industrial order into the entrepreneurial system. Faced with growing home-town responsibilities and the increased costs of keeping their immediate dependents at Agege, it is difficult to imagine that substantial numbers of established workers will be prepared to run the risks which such men as Akin and Abraham take at the present. Instead one might suggest that the current pattern of a trickle of workers into self-employment will be sustained. To put it another way, we are describing here a process in which the workers are being forced by the structure of their situation to accept life-time careers in factory work, a prospect which is anathema to them. This is a process of long term involuntary proletarianization, as opposed to the voluntary short term proletarianization which led to their initial participation in the industrial order of the Estate. But precisely because this is a novel and fluid setting, the workers' aspirations are not yet, as it were, entirely in tune with the limited opportunities which their situation affords them. As we have already indicated, most workers expect to spend between five and ten years in the Ikeja factories. As yet none have been in wage-employment for as many as ten years, and only a few for as many as five. This being so, they can continue to adhere to their aspirations for self-employment without especial inconsistency. They can be afflicted by despondency but not outright despair at their future circumstances. Within the space of a decade and perhaps less, the situation will, doubtless, be different. But this is to speculate.

There are two firm points to be made in conclusion. The first is that because of the relatively low wages which even established workers share, at present there is no opportunity for them to enjoy a reasonable life-style at the same time as saving with a view to self-employment. To retain the latter ambition, as they continue to do, is to exclude the possibility of using their income surpluses in the purchase of consumer commodities. The workers thus find themselves condemned to a limited life-style whilst, in ad hoc fashion, they add to their existing savings. The nature of the reward system on the Ikeja Estate is to this extent entirely inconsistent with both sets of expectations which the migrants bring to it. Second, and to conclude on a somewhat similar point to that of the previous chapter, the conditions which the workers find irksome and frustrating become all the more the subject of grievance against the background of metropolitan Lagos society in which a small but dominant minority enjoys exceptionally lavish life-styles and excellent life-chances. It is not so much inequality as such to which the workers object. As far as they are concerned, inequality between men is an inevitable development since they are born with different talents and develop contrasting levels of expertise over time. Rather it is the extent of inequalities, the vast nature of the gulf between rich and poor, with which they take issue, and the increasingly evident fact that this divide will be repeated in the next generation.

Thus far we have concentrated on the life-styles and life-chances of the workers themselves, and we will continue to do so. But it should not be completely ignored that as these workers begin to marry and have children, it is of growing concern to them that in the future they will have little to give to their children in order that they can get on in life. Since their wages are low, they anticipate considerable difficulties in properly educating their children. As the prospects of escape from factory work increasingly recede, they face what is for them the miserable prospect of an irrevocably low social rank which allows them neither dignity nor esteem. In the words of one worker:

> In aiming to become self-employed, I hope to become a man of moderate means. But also if I get to be a trader, my wife and my sons can be proud of me as well. If I remain as a worker, how is it possible that my son can be proud of me as his father? Not at all! For to be as a factory man is to be as a slave.

So, not only are the workers concerned to escape from their own poverty and low standing, they aspire to providing better prospects for their children. But the obstacles to both appear massive. By contrast, the next generation of those with wealth and power in southern Nigeria are going to inherit all the privileges of their fathers. Since Yoruba society has always been an open society with many opportunities for the poor to become better-off, the likely perpetuation of the present divide between rich and poor is a further development which leads the workers to become highly critical of the structure of the society at large. It compounds the deep-rooted grievances arising from their present shared circumstances.

4 Status and Class in Everyday Life

One of the themes I have been concerned to develop in previous pages is that an appreciation of the backgrounds of the migrant workers and the distribution of wealth and prestige in Agege is of central importance in explaining their profound dissatisfaction with their conditions of employment on the Estate. The combined influence of their experiences in these non-work social contexts is that the aspirations which migrants share are quite at odds with the life-styles and life-chances which the reward system of the Estate's factories allows them. Unlike the members of West European wage labouring forces, these West African workers have not as yet been socialized and coerced into accepting a subordinate wage-earning role for the entire duration of their working lives.[1] Because of the juxtaposition of the entrepreneurial economic order alongside the manufacturing system, and because in the former, as Agege people say, 'everyone is his own master', the workers have on hand an alternative system of socio-economic relationships which heightens the unacceptability of their class position in the factories. It is for these reasons that it would be erroneous to separate out the shopfloor workers from those other social contexts which are of importance to them. To consider them only as wage-earners in the context of the Estate would exclude from the analysis those ever present elements of comparison which compound the workers' natural sense of opposition to their subordinate status within the industrial order.

We can now turn to the social organization of the workers in their places of employment on the Estate. In changing the direction of the analysis in this way, the first requirement is to broaden the picture presented so far of the Ikeja labour force. The category of workers to which I am paying prime attention is the shopfloor men, but these manual workers must be considered in relation to other categories of wage-earners, especially skilled workers and white collar employees.

Occupational Stereotypes and Categorical Relationships

Occupational rank plays a significant part in the ordering of categorical relationships between workers. Quite apart from the interpersonal relationships which we have described so far, workers encounter one another in a variety of ephemeral social settings in which they do not come to know one another intimately yet are faced with the problem of ordering short-lived exchanges. It is in such situations that relationships are framed in terms of occupational stereotypes. Members of each occupational category share commonly-held understandings about members of the other two and they draw on these in order to guide social intercourse. The content of these stereotypes, (as opposed to their socio-economic bases which will be discussed later), is best indicated, I think, by linking together quotations gleaned from a diversity of social contexts.[2]

Consider first the stereotypes of others which are widely expressed by skilled workers, the foremen, chargehands, and supervisors in European companies. The following remarks are often made of white collar workers:

> Clerks are pen-pushers who always keep their hands clean . . . They are not real workers but paper-work men . . . If they were faced with a machine they wouldn't know what to do . . . They are young men with only books in their heads.

By contrast, skilled workers say of shopfloor employees:

> These are young men as we used to be . . . They work hard for low wages . . . The management exploits them more than anybody else . . . Some are good workers but they are too bothered with becoming independent men . . . They don't know the satisfaction of technical work because becoming self-employed is all they care about.

Status and Class in Everyday Life

The views held by clerical employees take the following forms. Of skilled workers they say:

They have worked themselves up from the shopfloor . . . They are like good craftsmen with talents in their hands . . . They deserve high wages and respect from shopfloor men . . . Supervisors have power but they rely on their hands and are not good at brainwork.

Their remarks on shopfloor workers are different again:

They are the really unfortunate ones . . . There was no money for their education . . . Their work is dirty and boring . . . Many are not intelligent and so they could not manage paperwork as we do . . . Some are lazy and so prefer to become self-employed where they can take things easy . . . The workers are at one with the union in the factory . . . They are exploited and have to fight.

When discussing foremen and chargehands the shopfloor workers say:

They have made their own way in factory life . . . They know more about the machines than the General Manager himself . . . Foremen have risen from the shopfloor but they now behave as if they are managers. Always they are concerned with production . . . Some of them are management men and they have forgotten how real workers at the bottom are suffering through factory work.

They view white collar workers as follows:

All they're concerned about is keeping clean their shirts and trousers . . . All day they sit on their backsides pushing pens around and dreaming of being managers . . . They have been lucky because their fathers had the money for all of their schooling . . . Clerks always come out being bossy and are not to be trusted because they are management men . . . They are parasites on our backs because they follow our union but they do it quietly . . . They are the ones who are really afraid of the managers.

Characterizations such as these will be well known to anyone with some acquaintance of a modern manufacturing context whether in a developed or underdeveloped society. Two features are significant about them. The first is that the members of each occupational category hold their own subjective rank order with the major index of rank being the particular valuable asset which they themselves share. According to their own system of ranking, the members of each category thus come out on top. In the case of skilled workers they are distinctive in having worked themselves up from the shopfloor. In doing so they have accumulated a vast amount of experience and technical expertise whilst remaining nevertheless manual workers in the strict sense. They get a good deal of personal satisfaction from these qualities, and on these counts they cannot be challenged by either clerks or shopfloor workers. For white-collar workers, their defining social characteristic and most valued asset is their level of formal education, which they frequently equate with superior intelligence. This becomes their key criterion for occupational rank. The shopfloor employees consider themselves to be 'real workers' not only because their work is manual but because they consider themselves to be the natural source of opposition to employers. By maintaining that both skilled workers and clerks are 'management men' they neatly invert by use of an epithet any status order which suggests that proximity to employers is a matter for pride and prestige. Their stereotypes emphatically deny such an assertion. Thus, occupational stereotypes reflect the contrasting conceptions of status within the factories, and allow members of each rank to claim the higher social status and enjoy some measure of self-esteem.

There are certainly threads of ambivalence within these stereotypes but, in so far as negative attributes and qualities are attributed to a particular occupational role, so the untoward behaviour of any individual incumbent of that role can be 'accounted for' with ease. In situations of an ephemeral or non-intimate nature, reference to what is generally expected of workers of particular rank can be used to explain away and defuse differences of opinion and judgement.[3] This occurs recurrently in both the factories and the Town. It emerges, for example, in the following exchanges extracted from workers' conversations in the canteen of an Ikeja factory. A shopfloor worker complained bitterly in the following terms to four of his workmates:

> That man Adekunle (a supervisor) acts just like the G.M. (General Manager) himself. He's a real management man. He told me to finish a job today which is really three days' work. He knows his machines but he pushes like dogs the men who work under him.

A shopfloor worker, following a visit to the administrative section of the factory, complained to his work peers of the clerk who had dealt with his request concerning his wage packet:

> He thinks he's a perm. sec. (i.e. Permanent Secretary) that fellow. He speaks English all the time but he does it so badly that I told him I didn't understand him. When he said I was a bushman, I told him to go back to school since he is only a small boy. These pen-pushers are all the same, education swells their heads.

So in the complex and often impersonal setting of the factory, unnecessarily formal and brusque behaviour underpinned by management-derived authority is explained away in terms of occupational stereotypes. A couple of brief illustrations drawn from settings in the Town make the same point. One shopfloor worker remarked to others that a clerk, their recently arrived co-tenant who had complained about the state of the compound latrine, should set about cleaning it himself. He added: 'Even a pen pusher should be able to do such handwork even though he might dirty his pants whilst doing it!', an innuendo which was much appreciated by his fellow workers. A shopfloor worker's wife who considered her neighbour to be acting in an increasingly stand-offish fashion, had it explained to her by her husband. The other's spouse, he noted, had recently been promoted within the administrative section; hence, perhaps the couple were 'becoming proud, like most clerks in the factories'. Occupational stereotypes developed in the industrial context are carried over into the urban situation and brought into play in order to declare inconsequential and unimportant actions which might otherwise be construed as anti-social and possibly offensive on a personal plane.

These stereotypes derive their continuing vitality and relevance from real divergences of material interests between those of different occupational rank. Among the different ranks there exist varying degrees of attachment to the industrial order, and these in turn relate to contrasting responses by those of different rank to the dominant cleavage in all the Ikeja factories, that between managements and wage-earners. We thus need to look more closely at the social characteristics and ambitions of skilled workers, white collar employees, and shopfloor men. This will lead to a rather crucial point concerning the shopfloor workers, namely that within the European factories they are faced with a marked degree of occupational immobility which ensures that they, unlike other employees, depend almost entirely on their house unions for any form of material advancement.

The Skilled Workers

The first significant factor concerning skilled workers is that most were amongst the initial cadres of employees taken on by European firms when these were established on the Estate in the early 1960s. The majority have worked for the same employers for six to eight years. The second is that in their early years of employment, for several reasons they were singled out for special training which has subsequently proved crucial in the development and unfolding of their occupational careers. They stood out from the majority of inexperienced workers because they had, before coming to Ikeja, already gained some experience and training as wage-earners in such locations as Apapa Port, the Ebute Metta Railway Compound, or establishments run by the United Africa Company (such as the Sapele Timber Works). Another reason was that, during the time they were labourers or general factory hands employed on basic construction work of the factory shells, they acquired patrons amongst European personnel who then promoted their interests.

These men were selected as special trainees: they were considered by their employers to be potential supervisory material and became the working apprentices of Europeans brought from Britain and elsewhere on contracts of varying duration. Where necessary they were also given special technical training in such establishments as the United Africa Company Training School in Lagos or the better technical colleges in the capital. As expatriate technical staff completed their contracts, the indigenous trainees who had performed most satisfactorily assumed vacant supervisory positions. The benefits to these men have been enormous for today, several years later, they share a wide-ranging technical expertise, which is why it is often said of them that 'they know more about machines than the G.M. himself'. Most have valuable trade certificates such as City and Guild qualifications. Since they were on the spot during the construction of factory buildings and the installation of machinery, they have a most extensive knowledge of workplace conditions, and a good deal of power is devolved to them by expatriate and indigenous management staff. Effectively, they have authority to hire, fire and promote the younger shopfloor workers below them. They are therefore both respected and feared, some having reputations which extend throughout the factories.

With monthly incomes ranging from around £N40 to £N70, these skilled workers can be termed the labour aristocracy of the Estate. By local standards they are affluent men indeed, and their relative prosperity is all the more noteworthy since they have spiralled up to their present rank in the space of the past decade. This in part also explains why most are only in their mid-thirties or early forties, a feature which assumes some importance, as we shall see, for those on the shopfloor.

Their work situation is highly favourable offering security, respect, authority and personal satisfaction.[4] So too is their wider market situation for they are much sought after by more recently established factories on the Estate or in its vicinity. New firms in the north Lagos area are often engaged in the manufacture of similar commodities to the longer-established European companies. If such men can be attracted away from their present places of employment, a new firm can immediately set them to work in training men on the shopfloor, rather than having to go through the time-consuming and costly exercise of initially training its own cadre of supervisory staff. Since in most firms, the wages of skilled employees comprise but a small proportion of total running costs, these new companies therefore offer higher than current supervisory wages in order to entice experienced men into their factories. The result is that foremen, charge-hands and the like, enjoy a continually improving market situation. The longer they remain where they are, and the more experienced they become, the higher the wage rates which new companies are prepared to offer them. It might be assumed that, in consequence, there would be a substantial movement of such men into these new firms, but turnover is slight and not sufficient to much affect the stability of the labour force at this level. Indeed skilled workers use the possible eventuality of making such a lateral move to press for higher wages in their existing places of employment. Their strategy is to request a rise from their employers at such times as appear appropriate, for example, following general wage increases at the shopfloor level, coupled with the suggestion that they are considering offers from other firms.[5] The important point is that they do so individually, not collectively, since each skilled worker has a particular expertise and a particular training.

By this individualistic bargaining tactic they try to take advantage of wider market circumstances. Of course the improvements they can realize are limited. This leads to the further consideration that maximizing their factory wages is not necessarily their utmost concern. What they especially value in their present places of employment is that they have been able to routinize their work lives to fit the pursuit of their entrepreneurial interests. Over the past few years, as their wages have risen, they have been able to establish business enterprises, consumer goods stores, bars, and even tenement buildings. A wife, an older son, or sometimes a kinsman runs the enterprise on a day to day basis, and the skilled worker spends whatever time he can there when he is off-duty. In effect, skilled workers have, or are beginning to enjoy, the best of both worlds. They have high wages on the Estate and their businesses in the Town. Were a skilled worker to move to a new company, this would inevitably require him to become acquainted with new machinery, spend more time travelling to his work place, and to take on much overtime work. The time spent on his private business would be correspondingly reduced.[6]

In more senses than one, therefore, are the skilled workers a labour aristocracy: they have relatively high incomes, excellent work and market situations, and the income from building up a trade store, owning a bar or putting up a tenement building. It is for these reasons that their circumstances have ramifications for younger shopfloor workers. Precisely because they can couple wage-earning with urban entrepreneurship, their career intentions are different from those of shopfloor employees. Whilst the latter wish to leave the factories as soon as possible, skilled workers anticipate remaining in factory employment until retirement age whereupon, with substantial long-term service payments, they will be able to further expand their business interests. Since such men are only in their thirties or forties, it is probable that they will remain in their privileged wage-earning roles for a further ten or fifteen years, and thus quite block promotion prospects for those below them. At the level of the shopfloor, the possibilities for individual advancement up the wage-earning scale therefore appear slight indeed.

Other factors compound this image of blocked mobility channels. It is of course the case that European companies are constantly expanding and that some skilled workers take advantage of higher wages in new companies, but the possible effects of these factors are minimized in several ways. First, available openings are few since the ratio of supervisory staff to shopfloor personnel is frequently in the region of 1:30 to 1:40. Second, the filling of new posts is in the hands of existing skilled workers. If one is not well-acquainted personally with such a worker, the chances of being considered for them are slight. Third, whilst five or ten years ago European firms had to make their own arrangements for training young skilled workers, increasingly Lagos technical colleges are providing lengthy apprenticeship courses. Certain Ikeja firms are recruiting these certificate holders since to do so is cheaper and more convenient than training apprentices on the shopfloor. This further compounds the limited possibilities for mobility from below.

So to some extent the social characteristics and ambitions of skilled workers iinfluence the circumstances of the majority of shopfloor employees. But to repeat, the skilled worker's assets are his work experience and technical expertise, and on these he must capitalize in order to push up his wages. As a result collective pressure and action in the form of trade unionism are of little value to skilled workers generally, and they stand aside from the processes of worker combination taking place on the shopfloor. Finally, in order that a skilled worker retains and builds upon his high value to his expatriate employers, he must add to his reputation for meeting production targets set by the management. Not surprisingly, whilst skilled workers are frequently respected for having worked their way up from the shopfloor, they are also labelled 'management men' who have 'forgotten how real workers at the bottom are suffering'.

White Collar Wage-Earners

White collar workers are, first and foremost, distinguished qualitatively from shopfloor workers by their level of formal education. Whilst the great majority of manual workers have only a primary or an incomplete secondary education, white collar staff have to have completed at least secondary school. This is an impenetrable barrier for those below, since there is no means whereby those with an incomplete education can put right the deficiencies in their backgrounds. But the differences between those of the two ranks are more wide ranging than this, and other factors lead to clerks developing their own distinctive patterns of accommodation to the division between managements and wage-earners.

The work situation of white collar workers is markedly different from that of other wage-earners. It is such as to compound the educated clerk's sense of superiority. Invariably the administrative sections of Ikeja factories are physically separate from buildings in which production takes place. Since white collar personnel are few in number they are concentrated in small office sections in which the work atmosphere is of a different order. European-style dress is *de rigeur* and English rather than Yoruba is the language spoken in most situations. Such considerations incline clerks to view themselves as quite distinct from ordinary workers. Another influence is that clerks' immediate superiors are generally middle-aged administrators who themselves began in wage-employment as secondary school leavers, and over the years have realized some mobility by acquiring further formal qualifications. Similarly the careers of personnel managers, sales managers and marketing men have frequently been advanced by further education whilst in wage-employment. Younger white-collar workers hope to emulate them and develop entire work careers in the factories.

To a considerable extent, these ambitions are fed by managerial policy. The range of white-collar incomes is substantial: expatriate managements pay their experienced and better-qualified staff as much as £N40 to £N70 per month. So, by contrast with shopfloor men, it is possible for clerks to rise up to lofty income levels, and encouragement to gain more paper qualifications takes several forms. These include the subsidizing of registration fees for higher courses, advances for the purchase of text-books, time off to attend lectures at approved colleges, and special leave in order to prepare for examinations. Above all, promotion up the administrative hierarchy is closely tied to passing the West African School Certificate, G.C.E. 'O' level and 'A' level examinations. Thus the reward system is geared to encouraging clerks to pursue industrial careers and it appears relatively successful in that they claim to be aiming at such occupations as accountant, personnel manager and sales manager. Part of the incentive also lies beyond their present places of employment since well-qualified administrators are in demand by new factories in Lagos and by oil companies, advertising and accountancy firms.

Yet there are weighty factors to counter-balance the influences which encourage clerks to consider themselves a class apart from the workers, by far the most significant being that most are not much better paid in their early years of factory employment. Inexperienced clerks receive only an additional £N5 to £N8 per month which, considering the costs and sacrifices involved in keeping them in school, is not a great deal. Not only do they have to compete with others of the same rank for management support for further education, but following part-time courses is not easily coupled with full-time factory work, for tenement rooms at Agege are scarcely conducive to study. The failure rate in examinations is high and this in turn increases overall costs. However ambitious they may be, clerks well recognize that advancing up the factory hierarchy is a long drawn out process.

The combined result of these factors is to place white collar employees in an invidious situation. They are pulled in one direction away from the manual workers by their subjective status, aspects of their work situation and their aspirations for the future. They are pulled in the opposite direction by their low wages, their subordinate rank in relation to employers, and the many obstacles to individual mobility. For the minority of better educated and better paid clerks the strategy is simply to keep in step with management expectations. As for the remainder, they try to effect an inevitably uneasy balance between keeping their options open for individual self-advancement, whilst looking to their house unions for collective improvement in conjunction with shopfloor men. Lower rank clerks incline towards house union membership, but they do not make their affiliation obvious by regular attendance at union meetings or seeking after union office. It is for these reasons that they are considered 'parasites' by shopfloor workers. Their uneasy position in relation to house unions is well demonstrated on the occasion of strikes. It is only when a shopfloor dominated movement is well underway that white-collar workers join in.

The Shopfloor and Collective Action

As one might expect from the foregoing, it is above all amongst skilled workers that one most regularly encounters expressions of job satisfaction. They are relatively affluent men or are in the process of becoming so. Their work involves a good deal of variation: and whilst its intercalary aspect involves them in some degree of conflict, they generally consider the negotiation of pressures from above and below to be of limited consequence when set against their growing technological expertise within their places of employment. What is especially revealing, perhaps, is that many define their work as a notably modern form of urban craftsmanship which, whilst it occurs in the factory situation and therefore has some of the stigma attached to wage-employment, nevertheless allows the development of technical skills, the ability to handle modern imported machinery and the opportunity to perform as a master would in relation to his apprentices in the wider entrepreneurial context. Likewise with white-collar workers one hears expressions of considerable satisfaction with the nature of their work, although the attractions which they attach to clerical employment are somewhat less tangible such as 'broadening the mind' and 'exercising one's intelligence'.

By contrast, the work of the shopfloor operatives allows of no similar benefits. Basic production processes are highly mechanized, tedious and mindless in their operation. Most work is carried out in large, noisy, sometimes dangerous, and usually very uncomfortable surroundings. Since much of their work is highly mechanized, there is little opportunity for workers to exercise any degree of initiative or control over the pace and nature of their work. There is little purpose in describing this at length. The point which should be emphasized is that the filling of beer bottles, the packaging of foam mattresses, the bagging of processed cocoa, or the painting of hundreds of enamelware bowls each day, all become especially dissatisfying by comparison with the satisfaction which workers consider to accrue to self-employed men. The latter are of course controlled by wider market forces: but they can to some degree choose the particular form of work which they undertake, they can set their own pace of work, and they can combine their individual production with some degree of involvement in the social life of the neighbourhood. It is these comparisons which shopfloor workers most regularly articulate rather than, for example, comparing the nature of their work with that of a white-collar employee. This deep-rooted intrinsic dissatisfaction with wage-employment is, of course, reinforced by their evident inability to realize any degree of individual mobility within the factories. Their level of education makes white-collar employment highly unlikely. The low turnover rate of skilled workers similarly means that they have little chance of selection for higher training.

Finally, whilst those above the level of the shopfloor are frequently improving their wider market situations, this is far from the case with shopfloor operatives: their market situation remains quite static. Whilst newly established firms attempt to attract experienced foremen and white-collar workers away from their present places of employment, these same employers recruit their shopfloor workers from the ranks of the unemployed; these can be trained quickly to perform elementary production tasks and be paid at the minimum wage-level. Under these circumstances there is nothing to be gained from those already in European firms attempting to move into other factories. In the light of these factors it is not surprising that the workers so frequently say: 'Once on the shopfloor, always on the shopfloor'. Nor is it surprising that the leadership and organization of their house unions are of great consequence, for as will by now be evident, the only way in which they can improve on their present income levels, and can foresee doing so in the future, is through collective pressure and collective action.

The Class Content of Everyday Life

Before turning (in Chapter 5) to patterns of institutionalized conflict between workers and managements, it is appropriate to now consider the recurrent expressions of class sentiment as they occur in the course of everyday life. For the Ikeja workers in general are continuously engaged in the elaboration of a distinctive working class ideology which provides the essential backdrop to intermittent action under the banners of the house unions. The central point I now wish to establish is that notwithstanding the variations detailed above, in the course of day to day experience Ikeja wage-earners acknowledge, in a variety of social forms, the major structured opposition of interests between themselves and managements.

It can of course be argued that the trade union movement is the most evident form of opposition to employers on the Estate, and strikes appear as the most obvious manifestation of this structured opposition of interests. I would suggest, though, that it is erroneous to approach these as the only manifestations of class opposition and that it would be mistaken to separate these out from the host of social milieux in which wage-earners are constantly elaborating an ideology of class opposition and resistance. Thus to digress for one moment, when the question is asked, as it increasingly is, whether urban African wage-earners comprise a working class and act like one, it is primarily answered by reference to the emergence, organization and efficacy of trade unions and the analysis of industrial and political disputes.[7] These are certainly very pertinent. Yet there is no reason why consideration should be restricted to such limited institutional forms and occasional events. At least this would be inappropriate for the present setting. Essentially, as a locale for modern capitalist manufacturing, the Ikeja Estate comprises a local level system of class relationships characterized by the dominant cleavage between those in control of productive resources and those who are not in control. Amongst the latter, the sense of opposition to employers finds expression in a variety of forms. Moreover, the articulation of shared class interests occurs not only in the factories, but in a multiplicity of social settings in which the experiences determined by their class position are actually lived out.

The first factor to stress is that the wage-earners operate in cognitive terms with an unambiguous two class folk model of the structure of the Estate. It rests on a straightforward dichotomy drawn between those who have power in the factories, their employers, and those who have not, the wage-earners in general. Unlike employment in, for example, government enterprises, there is in the Ikeja setting no difficulty in determining who takes the major decisions which affect workers' incomes and life-styles. Workers are aware that since the European firms are expatriate enterprises, their immediate employers may be ultimately responsible to higher authorities outside the country. But they assume, and rightly so, that the decisions of greatest importance to them are taken by the men on the spot, and that therefore the greatest collective pressure should be applied to General Managers.

Expatriate employers frequently try to render opaque the essential conflict of interests between those in control and those who are not. A number of the General Managers of major European firms are men of several decades' work experience in Nigeria; having developed a style of management considered appropriate to the colonial situation they present themselves as benign paternalists *vis-à-vis* their employees. But the transparency of this exploitative system of relationships does not lend itself easily to obfuscation and, as both Marx and Weber stressed, the transparency of any system of class relationships plays a key part in the development of lower class consciousness. Moreover the racial factor in the relationship between employers and employees has over the past few years been greatly mitigated by the indigenization of junior management posts. In European firms, the majority of such posts has been taken over by Nigerians. It is with these men that wage-earners come into contact rather than the small handful of expatriates who head the managerial hierarchy. Above all, the experience of work is such as to continually affirm that managements have a near-unassailable degree of power in the factory situation. While house unions have developed a considerable degree of effectiveness within European firms, work conditions still give rise to a pervasive sense of powerlessness. For the most part, workers have little opportunity to counter directives issued by managers; and when they are not responding to specific directives, they are controlled by the pace of the production line.

This conceptual polarization of management and workers is further reinforced by their complete separation beyond the work situation. As noted in Chapter 1, expatriate and indigenous managers reside either on the Ikeja Housing Estate or the Ikeja Government Residential Area to the south of the Industrial Estate. The symbolic properties of this topographic arrangement with Agege to the north could be scarcely equalled: in the words of one worker, 'The exploiters go south to Ikeja, the exploited north to Agege, and in the middle the place where we are exploited'. Furthermore the fact that all wage-earners, whether skilled, white collar or from the shopfloor, reside together in the Town is in certain respects a counter to the divisions of occupational rank as these find expression within the context of the Estate.

There is however rather more to it than this. Amongst the more privileged members of the Ikeja labour force there are singular interests in operation which further serve to promote the idea of oneness amongst wage-earners. For most white-collar workers this presents little problem since the majority of younger ones have incomes, and therefore life-styles, which only marginally distinguish them from shopfloor workers. Of more interest are the tactics adopted by skilled workers to counter the stigma of being labelled 'management men'. Skilled workers are very sensitive to being branded in this fashion: and so, in the Town, they enter into various strategies of image-management to stress that they are wage-earners with interests and concerns common to all. For example, they avoid drawing attention to the authority which they exert in the factory situation. Likewise they attempt to avoid unwarranted attention being drawn to their relative prosperity. In other words they assume a low profile in their respective neighbourhoods and stress their commonness with other employees. A good example of this was a young Ijebu foreman in my own neighbourhood who was aged only thirty-three and with an income of over £N60 per month was in the process of constructing a tenement building. For fear, as he put it, 'of everyone thinking I am a management man' he assumed a somewhat reserved posture in neighbourhood life. He dressed modestly, consciously avoided display of his relative prosperity, and in conversations with other workers was highly critical of managements and the authority system. In conversation he would frequently run down individual managers and openly discuss the necessity for shopfloor workers of engaging in strike action. As with other skilled workers, he constantly reiterated the fact that he had previously been a shopfloor man. Such strategies have their limits, but at all events it remains the case that skilled workers reside in the Town and can be classified as 'one of us' rather than 'one of them'.

In line with this conceptual polarization and the assumed incompatibility of management interests and wage-earners' interests which goes with it, the workers are constantly engaged in the elaboration of an ideology of opposition and resistance to employers, an ideology which declares legitimate most (if not all) action which opposes and undermines employers' authority. This ideology is captured in the language of battle and warfare which workers use to describe their relationships with their employers. Most workers' conversations about the factories contain such phrases as 'taking the fight to managers', 'bringing management to their knees', 'standing together to fight', and 'arming ourselves against employers'. They bring out the wage-earners' 'taken-for-granted' acknowledgement of the incompatibility of their interests and those of employers, and the assumption that outright conflict is part of the order of things on the Estate. Even amongst the most recent members of the Ikeja labour force, the metaphor of battle is widely-drawn upon. But there are other aspects of everyday life which contain this emphasis on opposition and resistance. Four are particularly worthy of note.

First there is the recurrent approval of minor acts which chip away at or, more strongly, undermine the authority of employers. Many such acts are relatively inconsequential in themselves: often they are no more than giving cheek to individual managers, making them appear foolish in front of other employees and cutting them down to size. Acts of outright insubordination and, above all, acts of industrial sabotage find the most ready and approving audience, for these highlight the ingenuity and resourcefulness of the workers involved. Most factories have their well known trouble spots from which industrial production across the shopfloor can be disrupted: the dye house of the textile factory, the bottling shed of the beer company, and the filling plants of paint firms, for example, are all foci for expressions of discontent; and it is from these that acts of sabotage have widespread repercussions. Thus within the bottling hall of the beer company, the fairly complex bottling machinery could easily be brought to a grinding halt and afford many workers some respite from the pressure of the production line. It is not however the acts themselves which are important so much as the generalized meaning which is attached to them. All become grouped together as individual or collective performances which are considered legitimate and justified by virtue of the sense of severe exploitation which workers feel.

Second, the ideology of resistance finds expression in the constant talk about trade union affairs and the social honour accorded to house union leaders. As we shall see in the next chapter, house unions are led from the shopfloor and are very much geared towards the interests of shopfloor workers. As a result the wage-earners are constantly involved in comparing house unions with one another. They demonstrate their attachment to these organizations by vigorously championing them and building up their reputations in a most spirited fashion. So too with their house union leaders, and in particular union presidents. As noted in an earlier chapter, in Agege wealth and prestige are concomitants. Only the more affluent entrepreneurs are accorded high social standing in all quarters, including the factory workers. The major exceptions to this general rule are the house union leaders. Whilst they are workers with much the same life-styles as the majority of their followers, nevertheless the deference accorded to them by the workers is considerable. They are judged to be altruistically-inclined men who assume arduous roles for the same material gains which they realize for other members. In the tenement buildings and neighbourhoods where they live, they are frequently turned to for advice and assistance, and are often called upon to settle disputes between younger workers. They are invited as honoured guests to the meetings of workers' small clubs, as well as their marriages, and the naming ceremonies of older workers' newborn children. House union presidents are symbolic figures of resistance and opposition to Ikeja employers and as such they are accorded extensive public respect.

What is especially significant here is that the workers are exhibiting a distinctly proletarian normative system in the Town. As has been stressed, the factory workers are a numerical minority in Agege, a community which stresses the values of urban entrepreneurship, competitive individualism, self-help, individual striving and the realization of personal goals and interests. By contrast, the shared ideology of the wage-earners *vis-à-vis* the Estate is one which stresses solidarity and unity, collective action, and the subsuming of individual goals under the general advancement of shared interests, all of which are enshrined in the existence of the house unions and the union presidents who lead them. For self-employed men and women in the Town, these cultural emphases are irrelevant if not meaningless. Middle-aged entrepreneurs by contrast with the factory workers, consistently deny that union presidents are to be accorded social deference and have little time for them. As one entrepreneur-landlord once put it in conversation with several of his wage-earning tenants: 'These union presidents who you praise so often, they are nothing to people like me. They spend all their time organizing hundreds of workers, yet all they get out of it is the same money as everyone else'. It is in this sense one can speak of the wage-earners being engaged in the expression of distinctive socio-cultural forms. These provide them with a particular code of normative behaviour which contrasts with the dominant ethos of Agege community. It separates them out from the mainstream culture and matches well their particular social and economic circumstances.

Third, and the obverse of the second point, severe social sanctioning is brought to bear in the Town on individuals who are known or considered to have broken this normative code. In part the severity of such sanctioning is reflected in the fact that few have transgressed it, but on occasion men have crossed the picket lines when strikes were underway. The stigma of the blackleg has remained with them ever since. The greatest opprobrium is reserved for men who have performed disreputably as union leaders, a case in point being one man who had led a strike in a Chinese enamelware factory. In this sector of factory employment the workers' frustration at not being able to form their own house unions periodically explodes into sudden wildcat strikes followed by the hurried election of leaders. These desperate tactics usually prove unsuccessful since non-European employers, after initially recognizing the leaders in order to have production resumed, then carry out a steady war of attrition against them. In the late 1960s in the company to which I have just referred, such a wildcat strike took place, and the man in question was elected president of the embryonic union. Shortly afterwards, rather than being sacked as usually happens, he was promoted to foreman, a position which he accepted: it was also rumoured that he was given a lump sum by his employers. The subsequent costs to him were enormous. He was abused inside the factory and on the streets of the Town, and neighbourhood life became quite intolerable for himself and his family to the point at which he moved from the Town altogether. This was an extreme case but as we shall see, other leaders appear to have used union office as a stepping stone to mobility within their places of employment. These men are not subject to the same torrent of public abuse, yet in the factories and the Town the scandal surrounding their careers is widely disseminated behind their backs and occasionally comes to the surface.

Fourth, the ideology of opposition and resistance finds expression in a particular folk-lore which incorporates the types of action described above. Events which are considered of singular importance and merit become incorporated into a core set of traditions which become revamped and reworked as time passes. Clearly I use the term 'traditions' in a loose sense since this is a recently established wage-labour force. While most of the concerns referred to so far have a currency only amongst limited segments of the labour force (e.g. an act of sabotage assumes its greatest relevance in the factory setting in which it took place), certain key events become of relevance to all in symbolizing the need for opposition and unity.

The outstanding example is the 1964 General Strike which was a turning point in the history of industrial relations on the Estate. This was the first occasion on which workers stood in collective opposition to their employers and the civilian government of the time. Older factory hands frequently recall it in the most vivid terms to more recently arrived members of the labour force. In 1971 when the workers were engaged in outright conflict with their employers and the military government, 1964 was considered by many workers to have established an important precedent for this later conflict. It functioned in effect as a paradigm for appropriate action and was looked upon as part of a tradition of opposition to exploitation which had to be kept up. Since this will be referred to in Chapter 6, it will not be detailed here.

In sum, the wage-earners operate cognitively with a clear cut two class model of employers on the one hand and workers on the other. In a variety of ways they articulate the inevitable opposition which follows from the incompatibility of the interests of both sides. They also adhere to a proletarian ideology which constantly legitimates expressions of opposition. In the light of this model and these established emphases all of which are taken as 'given' by the workers, in the course of everyday life new events and issues become incorporated into this system of mutually shared understandings. These become interpreted in a particular way to accord with the workers' existing cognitive framework and in turn reinforce the relevance of these beliefs in such a way that their ideology seems to become a 'closed' or 'sealed-off' one. To use a well known anthropological distinction, the established system of beliefs is subject to primary and secondary elaboration.

Of this, one brief example must suffice. It concerns a young shop-floor worker, Sule, who found himself in the highly privileged position of being selected for further training as a loom overlooker in the textile company where he worked. The course lasted some three months in all and Sule did relatively well in the various examinations conducted by the management. But they operated a rule that, following training, newly promoted loom overlookers had to spend a further three months proving their skilled expertise on incomes below the usual rate for the job. A few weeks previously, a new textile company on the Ilupeju Industrial Estate south of Ikeja had begun to advertise for skilled workers and was offering higher wages than those current in Sule's company of employment. So, shortly before the training course was to end, Sule took a day's leave, went through certain tests of his new skills, and was offered a permanent position in the new company on a monthly income well in excess of the one in the firm which had trained him. He then tendered his resignation, intending to take a short holiday with the long-service gratuity to which he was entitled after some six years of factory work. His employers however were adamantly opposed to this. They attempted to sack him on the grounds that during training he had performed incompetently and was no longer considered a desirable employee. If this move had been successful, Sule would have lost the gratuity to which he was entitled. But with the support of his house union secretary, Sule was able to show from office records that he had done well during the training period. Faced with the threat of union action on the grounds of wrongful dismissal, the management's case collapsed, Sule was fully paid off, and eventually he became a well-paid chargehand under his new employers.

This is to reduce to bare outline a complicated sequence of events. The course of action, however, was straightforward. In essence an individual worker in a relatively privileged position, attempted to capitalize on the favourable market situation which is, as we have seen, a feature of those with particular technical training and skills. Being a young man rather than a well established middle-aged worker it was to his advantage to exploit the opportunities afforded him. Since he had no sense of loyalty or obligation to the firm, he simply took up the best career prospects available.

Yet amongst his co-workers and urban acquaintances, the interpretations placed on Sule's performance contained a quite different stress. Over the next two weeks or so, it became evident that his actions had taken on a very distinctive set of meanings as news about him had become widely disseminated. In his neighbourhood Sule encountered a number of co-workers: from repeated references to his resignation it became evident that it had been widely discussed across the shopfloor. Furthermore, via various gossip sets extending from the factory into the Town, wage-earners from other companies had heard of it too. In short, it had become something of a *cause célèbre*.

More than this, the workers had read into the episode particular interpretations which were quite incidental to Sule's own aim. For example, several workers expressed to him their satisfaction that he had 'cheated the management'. They were thus drawing on the presumed position of Sule's employers that, having invested money and time in his training, they expected some return from his enhanced skills. By resigning and moving to another company, Sule was considered to have denied them any such return. Other workers implied in their comments that he had effectively turned the table on his employers. As a subordinate by virtue of his class position, under normal circumstances Sule was relatively powerless. Ironically, by training him as a skilled worker, a strong bargaining position had been created for him by his employers. In the words of one acquaintance: 'You have been able to exploit the management just as they usually exploit us'. Other workers went further than this: as one put it, 'It is good to know a man who has been able to tell the management to go to hell!' The common aspect to all workers' responses however was that Sule's performance was a rebellious act. It was one which openly challenged the authority of the employers and defied their degree of control in a manner which can be but rarely achieved by the wage-earners. By stressing this particular aspect of the sequence of events, the workers attached a special symbolic meaning to it. Furthermore, by so doing the workers, in effect, created an event in which they could vicariously share and gain considerable satisfaction. All connected with Sule expressed full approval for the way in which he had cocked a snook at his employers. By upstaging the latter, Sule was considered to have earned his peers' approval for an action which in terms of their proletarian ideology was entirely legitimate. To repeat, in many respects the importance which the workers attached to Sule's performance was scarcely warranted and was not the interpretation which the subject himself placed on his actions. The major point is that in a social context such as this, where the majority

Status and Class in Everyday Life

of workers adhere to a class model of their local situation and expound a normative code of opposition and unity, then even a relatively innocuous act such as the one described assumes a singular symbolic importance. It is incorporated into an existing mode of interpretation and defined in such a way as to reinforce that mode further.

Conclusion

The themes developed in the previous section will be quite familiar to readers acquainted with the social and cultural frameworks of West European wage-earners. A conceptual framework which clearly divides managements and workers into opposed categories, the stress on resistance to employers as being of the natural order of things, and the interpretation of particular events in such a manner that they fit existing modes of interpretation, all these are recurrent in anthropological and sociological accounts of the working classes in modern industrial societies.[8] To this extent we can say that the Ikeja workers have a sense of class consciousness. Taking the chapter as a whole, there are two further points to be established.

The first of these is that inter-relationships between workers of different occupational rank are frequently characterized by ambiguities and inconsistencies. To some extent this is reflected in the shared occupational stereotypes with which the chapter began. These inconsistencies will be especially evident by now since, whilst latterly we have argued that the workers articulate an ideology of unity between themselves, it has also been established that workers respond in quite different ways to the distribution of power within the Ikeja factories. It is only the shopfloor workers, however, who respond to the dominant cleavage between employers and employees on a consistently collective basis. By contrast, white-collar and skilled wage-earners break ranks and pursue their interests on an individualistic basis. The resulting ambiguities reflect the fact that, despite their all being wage-earners, the division of labour is such as to ensure that those of different rank have different material interests.

These emerge in a diversity of ways with perhaps the most marked inconsistencies surrounding the position of the skilled workers. Within the context of the factories they exert a good deal of authority over the workers and become labelled 'management men': yet in the context of the Town they stress that gains have to be wrested from employers by collective action — and sometimes proffer advice as to the most effective course strike action might take. Likewise amongst the white-collar workers, performances which are separately embarked upon appear distinctly at odds when set against one another. For example, they are engaged in strenuous efforts to create careers for themselves in the factories in order to become auxiliaries to senior managers: yet when industrial disputes break out, they frequently follow the lead taken by shopfloor men in manifest opposition to employers. The same anomalies occur amongst shopfloor workers in relation to those of different rank. Whilst at times they dismiss the clerks as 'parasites', when these join the ranks of striking shopfloor men, the latter welcome them into their number since it gives their house union leaders all the more bargaining power in relation to their employers.

The second point to be stressed is that despite the fact that workers pursue their respective sectional interests through different strategies of accommodation to the industrial order, the members of different occupational ranks do not in any sense hamper or impede the progress of those in other ranks. The different courses whereby skilled workers, clerks, and shopfloor men seek to advance their material interests are quite complementary with one another. In no sense does the individualistic response of, say, the skilled worker militate against shopfloor employees gaining wage increments and other improvements through collective action. Rather to the contrary, as a general rule, once increments have been won through collective action on the shopfloor, skilled workers and higher paid white collar employees press for corresponding increases on similar grounds.

So it is only amongst the shopfloor workers that the ideology of class is fully translated into collective action. What is of further advantage to them is that they can do so without particular reference to developments which are going on elsewhere within the factory hierarchy. On a comparative basis, this situation is thus somewhat different from that which has often developed elsewhere amongst African wage-labour forces. A recurrent feature in other studies of worker combination is the struggle for control over trade union organizations between skilled workers, educated white collar employees and manual operatives.[9] Such conflicts have often resulted in union movements being seriously weakened, and, more often than not, the interests of ordinary workers have suffered in consequence. The situation on the Estate contrasts with this in that shopfloor workers' interests can dominate by default of the others. Since neither skilled nor white-collar employees have an unqualified attachment to trade unionism, this is a context in which the trade union movement can be fully oriented to the protection and advancement of the interests of those at the base of the industrial order. Within the Ikeja setting, the field of trade unionism is left open to those who depend most on these organizations.

5 Unions, Leaders and Followers

In this chapter and the next, I am concerned to discuss the organization of the Ikeja house unions, the characteristics of their respective leaderships, the relationships between union leaders and their followers, and the effectiveness of these organizations in relation to expatriate employers. It will be quite evident from previous chapters that the shopfloor workers in European firms are greatly dependent on the house unions and their leaders. In the words of one worker: 'Your union and your union president are as your brothers in the Town. Without your union you are as nothing for no one else can protect you against the management and the government'. He went on to say, quite rightly, that this was so whether a worker was concerned about improvements in his immediate style of life or his chances in the future of becoming self-employed. At first sight this appears a fertile field for worker combination. To what extent, then, is the organization of trade unionism suited to taking full advantage of the situation and to bringing tangible gains to the workers? By way of introduction to this chapter and the next, two points are of critical importance and need to be borne in mind throughout.

The first of these is that the Ikeja house unions are very recently formed organizations. Although in formal terms the house unions were set up in the first half of the 1960s, it was not until the second half that they began to make their presence felt. It is only over a short period of time that the wage-earners have moved from a position characterized by disorganization to one of noteworthy organization and representation *vis-à-vis* employers. This being the case, the workers do not merely assess the value of trade union membership in terms of the immediate material gains but in terms of job security, improvements in work circumstances, the opportunity to debate union tactics, and so on. To put it a different way, the factory workers evaluate the return from trade union membership in terms of what has been achieved in the recent past as well as what is being achieved in the present. These workers are pragmatic and when they say, as they frequently do, 'We have come a long way in a short period of time', they are also recognizing that any amelioration in their conditions is a drawn out process in which there are no easy routes to collective improvement. A good deal has been achieved in recent years and of this the workers are especially proud.

The second important point is that the house union system is an inevitable and unavoidable product of the structure of industrial production on the Estate as it has evolved during the nineteen sixties. From the beginning, each factory has been developed as a separate system of production. A diverse range of commodities is produced, each requiring different raw materials, a particular technology and its own sales and distribution system. Moreover, not only are the factories autonomous units, they deploy, grade, pay and reorganize their workers in markedly different ways. This being so, there has never really existed the possibility of the workers combining into a unified labour movement in opposition to the employer class as a whole.[1] The far more rational response has been the development of house unions in which each labour force in a single factory combines in opposition to its respective management, thereby taking advantage of workers' concentration in the same factory compound and their sense of opposition to the same employer. It is the best possible adaptation to the distribution of management power on the Estate, and the compartmentalization of production thus ensures that the Ikeja labour movement has a highly segmented form. The argument to be developed in this chapter is that whilst, at the local level this leads to the house unions having certain strengths which leaders can exploit, its segmented form is a point of intrinsic weakness. Their separation from one another militates against their combining in relation to the government, a requirement which has become especially pressing in the light of recent political and economic developments beyond the level of the Estate.

For the moment let us concentrate on the social organization of the house unions in the European firms and describe some of the changes which have occurred within them. In order to appreciate the significance of these it is necessary to see them in the light of the recent past. This requires us to go back to the early 1960s when the European firms initially began production.

The Development of Trade Unionism

In the early 1960s not only were the Ikeja labour forces small, they were distinctly unamenable to any form of combination. The majority of workers were young men in their late teens or twenties, recent migrants from their home towns lacking in any prior experience of wage-employment or trade unionism. Above all, their employment was exceptionally insecure. Most were employed as daily or weekly paid labourers engaged in the construction of factory buildings or the clearing of the land. Others were taken on to provide the manual labour for installing imported machinery under the supervision of expatriate engineers. As a result of various difficulties and setbacks, such as the late arrival of machinery or poorly co-ordinated work schedules, these workers were continually being laid off only to find themselves re-employed shortly afterwards by the same company or a different one. Moreover, their goal was to be taken on to the production lines of the factories once these were properly underway, a consideration which required the workers to keep their heads down.

Even after workers were employed on a more regular basis the prospect of being sacked for 'making trouble' proved a major obstacle to combination. In most factories, though, there appears to have been a distinct minority of workers who had been wage-earners before coming to Ikeja and who initially mooted the idea of trade unionism. They had worked, for example, in the railway compound at Ebute Metta, Apapa Port, or for one of the expatriate trading companies in Lagos. Consequently, they had at least some acquaintance with trade union organization as well as wage-employment. The general pattern seems to have been that they raised the idea of trade unionism in a tentative fashion with their fellow workers but had found them essentially unresponsive. As one such individual recalled (he was an ex-railwayman):

> Everyone was interested when you talked to them. But to have a union meeting to get things underway — that was impossible. Everyone was thinking at the time, 'If I join a union then I will be terminated'. So all we did was talk and nothing happened.

This situation prevailed until 1964 when a complete transformation of the industrial scene occurred following the General Strike of that year. In 1963, a year of considerable political turbulence, the heads of several of the country's national trade union congresses united together to demand a government enquiry into wage-levels in both the public and private sectors. The government's response was to establish a Wages and Salaries Review Commission under Mr. Justice Adeyinka Morgan. In April of the following year, the Morgan Commission presented its recommendations to the government.[2] It quickly became common knowledge that these included increases for most low-paid wage-earners. The report was also critical of the many inequalities in Nigerian society at large. For this reason the government delayed publication of the report for one month, and on its eventual publication there was no accompanying White Paper setting out the official government position. The Joint Action Committee of labour congress leaders took advantage of the resulting frustration and anger to call a General Strike. This was overwhelmingly supported and lasted for two weeks. The outcome was a general upward revision of wage-levels.[3]

It was in the aftermath of the General Strike that the Ikeja house union movement took off, breaking the vicious circle of earlier years. The workers had responded to the call of the Joint Action Committee. As one striker recalled: 'For the first time, we could see the managements were just as afraid of us as we had been of them'. Most important of all, the workers felt that at this time no expatriate management would dare sack employees who now joined a trade union, since to do so would be a politically provocative act. A crucial part was played by those workers referred to earlier with some prior experience of trade unionism. In most firms it was these men who seized the initiative, rallied the workers on the shopfloor of their respective factories, arranged the first union meetings, and the election of union officers. Having done so, they were also elected to union office since, being somewhat experienced, they were evidently best suited to lead. As an inexperienced worker recalled his first union meeting:

> We knew we had to get the union underway because the managers were exploiting us so badly in those days. You never knew from one day to the next whether you had a job to go to. But with the General Strike behind us we knew we wouldn't be sacked. The management wouldn't dare ... Most of us didn't know what we were doing really. There were so few of us who knew what trade unionism was about. So when those who had an inkling said 'Let's start a union', then we all went along and voted the same men (into office) as well.

Notwithstanding these promising beginnings, after 1964 the progress of the house unions was both slight and slow. Certain of the early leaders were notably active in the education of their members. One went so far as to organize a weekly evening class, whilst others issued broadsheets and circulars explaining how unions might best be run. All of them began to enter into negotiation with their respective employers. Yet it is clear from available records, as well as oral accounts, that their demands were modest ones. They concerned such issues as safety, canteen facilities, and the opportunity for workers to have some choice as to when to take their holidays. They did not for the most part focus on the important issues of job security and wage-levels; and even when these were raised, employers appear to have had little difficulty in setting them on one side without provoking any reaction. Considering how important these issues were to the shopfloor men, this is difficult to account for. Union leaders of this period told me that it was because they were inexperienced and unsure of their members. They felt that a more militant line which headed for confrontation with employers might result in the destruction of the unions should the workers begin to waiver. Somewhat more influential than their sense of caution appears to have been the constant jostlings for union control within elected house union executives. Particularly in the period 1964 to around 1967, most union leaders seem to have spent a good deal of time accusing one another of corruption and nepotism as well as the personalizing of union offices. Whatever the reasons for the proliferation of these disputes, the important point is that these were invariably conservative leaders. After two or three years of unionism in the European firms, the gains to the workers had been slight.

By contrast, in the period after approximately 1967, the situation in the European factories changed considerably. In these later years of the decade some of the strengths of the house union system were realized, and under a quite different set of leaders to previously. These were new men who generally promised a more militant style of leadership aimed at tangible gains for their followers. One factor here was that during the previous period there had developed a prevalent dissatisfaction with the performances of those elected to office after 1964. This was partly because of the lack of improvements, but there had been further issues. One was that some house union presidents and vice-presidents had developed close ties with the national labour congresses in Lagos. To their followers, they appeared to be more committed to these organizations than the house unions they were supposed to be leading. For example, two house union leaders became quasi-officials in these labour congresses to the apparent neglect of their house union duties.

The other and more common issue was that within their places of employment, union leaders had become occupationally distinct from the bulk of their followers. In a number of instances they had received promotions which put them somewhat ahead of most union members on the shopfloor. As we have said, the founders of these organizations were not only experienced in trade unionism, they were also wage-earners before joining the Ikeja factories. As their firms had expanded and new junior supervisory positions became available, some of the union leaders were promoted into them. Indeed a few were eventually destined to become the skilled workers or well-paid white-collar workers of the present day, i.e. members of the Estate's labour elite. At the time, this longer term result does not appear to have been clear. Nevertheless, it was apparent that union leaders were doing somewhat better in career terms than most of their members.

The outcome of these developments was considerable disenchantment on the shopfloor followed by upheaval. In almost all the European factories incumbent leaders were accused of using their offices as vehicles for personal advancement, and this in turn appears to have affected their efficacy. Clearly this could not be tolerated for long, and a number of subsequent developments have carried through to the present time. One of these was that at annual general meetings new leaders emerged to displace office incumbents. These were popular shopfloor men who were able to mobilize existing currents of discontent. They were also men who appeared unlikely to manipulate their positions as their predecessors had done. (Of this, more in a moment.) In certain instances the changeover was fairly peacefully effected although not without much prior politicking. In one house union for example, the incumbent president declared his intention not to stand again since his invidious position had provoked considerable adverse comment. Before joining the labour force he had had several years in wage-earning. Once in the factory, he had enjoyed some minor promotions over three years, but in his final year as union president he had had two major promotions to a middle range supervisory rank making somewhat absurd his holding elected office. In other house unions the changeover of leadership proved traumatic and disruptive as incumbent officers attempted to retain their posts despite a general feeling on the shopfloor that they were no longer suitable.

Another development was that, in order to distinguish themselves entirely from their predecessors with their apparent lethargy and conservatism, the new men committed themselves to bringing major changes in the style of leadership, to enhance workers' job security, gain wage-increases, and to engage in militant action where necessary. Of course most leaders in union settings engage in somewhat similar claims during their campaigns for office, but for the new men in the late 1960s it was imperative for them to make some headway on these fronts. Not only had they linked earlier union conservatism to the suggestion that it was a product of their predecessors' self interest: by driving them from office, the new men created precedents for their own removal if they did not bring some benefits to their followers. Most of these leaders effected some marked changes, but it is worth stressing that it was essential for them to do so in order to ensure their own survival. One union president who came to office in 1968 and, as his followers recall, in doing so vilified his predecessor, summarized his situation in the following way:

> As soon as I was elected, I knew I had to meet my promises. That is why I have taken some risks. I had promised that jobs would be made properly secure and that we would get increments for those on the lowest wages. And then I'd talked about striking as well. The workers wanted some improvements and I knew that if the advancement did not come I would not last long as president ... otherwise I too would be out at the next election.

This then is the historical background to the house unions and the leaders of the present. It is an oversimplified picture, for within the unions there have been particular developments specific to each. Nevertheless it is a reasonable description of the overall pattern of union emergence by 1967 to 1968. The most salient points to emerge are that previous leaders were discredited by virtue of having become separated from the shopfloor, there had been a lack of improvement during their terms of office, and the present leaders came to power on the strength of committing themselves to change. With these points in mind, we can turn to the house unions and their leaders as they stand today.

The Leadership and Organization of the House Unions

The table indicates the more important characteristics of two current

Two House Union Executives

Education	Occupational Rank	Age	Wage £N per month	Length of Service (years)
International				
Secondary 2	Shopfloor	31	22	6
Secondary 2	Shopfloor	28	19	6
G.C.E. 'O'	Clerical	29	31	4
Secondary 4	Shopfloor	28	25	3
Secondary 5	Clerical	29	30	3
Standard 5	Timekeeper	35	32	6
Secondary 5	Shopfloor	32	26	5
Secondary 4	Shopfloor	29	22	4
Champion				
Primary 6	Shopfloor	29	18	6
Secondary 3	Shopfloor	29	28	4
G.C.E. 'O'	Clerical	30	37	3
Secondary 3	Shopfloor	28	27	4
Standard 4	Timekeeper	35	24	5
Secondary 5	Shopfloor	25	16	2

house union executives: International, a textile company which is also the largest Ikeja factory with some 3000 workers, and Champion, a beer producing firm of more average size with a little over 800 employees. All of these men occupy unpaid elected office.[4] Their social characteristics are quite typical of trade union leaders in the European companies on the Estate.

Shopfloor workers predominate. Within International, five out of eight executive members are drawn from the shopfloor: in the case of Champion, four out of six are manual operatives. Shopfloor dominance is not complete. Each union has some white-collar representation with a lower ranking clerk filling the post of internal secretary. This is the norm in the unions since the position involves extensive note-taking, the occasional publishing of newssheets and the handling of union accounts. Both unions have a timekeeper on the executive committee, though the particular occupation is of somewhat less significance than the age and length of work experience. They are older than their fellows and considerably older than most ordinary workers. This too is a recurrent feature, and it arises because workers feel that the presence of such men gives their unions a degree of respectability and authority which they might otherwise lack. As with all leadership groups, however, the degree of involvement and influence in decision making varies between executive members. In these two groups as with others, the shopfloor workers are the men who are really influential and comprise the inner core of decision makers.

A further point about these elected officials is that they are workers with rather more factory experience than most of their members. Length of service indicated on the table refers to years in their present place of employment, but several had been in one other firm beforehand. They are thus men well acquainted with the industrial order, and this in turn relates to their being slightly older than most wage-earners. What is of special significance is that whilst their income levels are above the average for shopfloor workers, this is primarily a result of their length of service: that is, they have gained the annual increments which accrue to all workers. Apart from the occasional grade promotion, they have benefitted no more than most workers from wage employment. Equally important is the fact that it is unlikely they will gain any particular or out of the ordinary improvements in the future since, as with the great bulk of workers, they have incomplete secondary educations, with the exception, of course, of the two clerks. Thus these are workers drawn from the shopfloor who are destined to remain there. As such they are fully representative of the shopfloor workers who elected them into office.

Finally, and most important of all considering the influence which they wield, the two presidents of the house unions illustrate the same characteristics. These are the men first listed in each case. Akanale, the president of International, has worked for some six years in the factory, all of which have been spent in the same section. Whilst somewhat older than most workers, his monthly wage is but £N22; over the years he has received only annual increments to his income. As can be seen, his level of education is low and effectively rules out any possibility of mobility up the factory hierarchy: this the experience of the past strikingly confirms. Bankole, the president of the Champion house union is in a similar situation. He too has been employed in the factory for six years, but his especially low income is partly explained by a break in his service in the factory. His level of formal education is the minimal one for gaining entry into factory employment, and makes quite negligible his prospects for any form of in-factory mobility.

The workers thus elect to representative office men who are much the same as themselves. The only respects in which they are different, for example in length of service, are in qualities which make them especially suitable as spokesmen for the majority of shopfloor members. The major contrast with the past is that the most important figures, the house union presidents, are highly unlikely to develop any interests or ambitions not shared with their memberships at large. They are not men who can use their offices as stepping stones to mobility within the workplace.[5] This alone is sufficient for most workers to consider that an important break has been made with the past.

Turning now to the organization of the house unions, a number of changes have been brought about under the leadership of the new men. In earlier years most functions were carried out by elected union presidents and one or two of their closest associates. They made few attempts to involve the labour force at large in decision-making. Many workers who were union members in the mid-1960s say that they had little idea of day to day developments unless leaders were disputing among themselves. Still less were they involved in what most workers understand, open elections apart, as the democratic process, — a regular opportunity to publically support or veto policies put forward by their leaders. By contrast, the new men do run their organizations in an open and democratic fashion, in part as a means of avoiding the widespread dissatisfaction of earlier years.

There are several ways in which they have done this. First, simply because they are on the shopfloor working alongside their members, they are constantly on hand for conversation and discussion of current problems. Second, in conjunction with the support provided by other executive members, the new men have attempted to establish a system of shop-stewards who are able to relay specific issues as well as general opinions to their respective leaders. Since most labour forces are relatively small, and divided between three shifts, this requires only half a dozen or so stewards, along with executive members, to provide a reasonably comprehensive coverage. Not only does this ensure that union leaders are sensitized to prevalent opinion, the members are generally afforded proper protection of their interests. If a worker considers he is not being paid the proper rate for the job or if he is being victimized by a supervisor, he has on hand a union representative to whom he can quickly turn for support. To this extent, current house union organization takes full advantage of the concentration of members within the single factory.

Third, as part and parcel of their democratic style, union presidents convene general meetings several times each year, and at times of dispute perhaps two or three in quick succession, in order that ordinary workers may voice their opinions. Within these, they can freely express their opinions and indeed take the initiative in proposing tactics for the executive to adopt. Most issues are put to a formal vote. It should be noted that under normal circumstances, i.e. where there are no contentious issues on hand, attendances are low, usually between 10 per cent to 15 per cent of those eligible. They are held on a Sunday afternoon in a local hotel at Ikeja, and as a result conflict with the period of the week in which workers make visits home or to friends elsewhere in Lagos.[6] Workers frequently argue that as major issues are extensively discussed on the shopfloor, attendance at the meetings is somewhat unnecessary. Be that as it may, those who do turn up have the opportunity to assess their leaders and union policies critically. Doubtless some are inhibited from speaking by the fact that English is the language of general meetings. This is the pattern on the grounds that Yoruba dialect variations would introduce an undesirable ethnic element into settings which must be free of such influences.[7] But whilst they may be thus inhibited, they are nevertheless able to scrutinize their leaders and their performances. So, once again the position contrasts with three or four years ago: the unions have been opened up in such a way as to encourage grassroots participation.

Finally, to turn to the most important area of all, house union membership has brought certain tangible gains over the past three years or so, especially to shopfloor members. As noted earlier, until the late 1960s the achievements realized by the first coterie of union leaders were relatively slight. Although they did at least gain formal recognition, their demands were modest and not backed by the threat of concerted action. There appear though to have been several major issues which led to growing disenchantment. One was that whilst the unions were formally recognized, employers made major changes without consultation with, or opposition from, incumbent union officers. Another was that employers sacked workers for their low output, for engaging in disputes with supervisors and so on, without the unions exercising their right to be consulted. Above all, there had been no advancement on the crucial issue of wages. On all of these considerations, albeit in varying degree, the present day leaders have made some headway.

For a start, house union leaders are now consulted by employers on major changes pending within their factories, a development which has been won by their taking the initiative. Rather than waiting to be consulted (the earlier norm), on coming to power the new men insisted on their right to representation, and over the past couple of years they have settled on various test cases to emphasize that they are instigating new regimes. For example as it became evident that employers were intending the reorganization and reallocation of workers inside the factories, leaders moved quickly to become involved in these decisions. This change of leadership style has been fully recognized by employers, not least because the new men have threatened go-slows and more concerted action if the right to consultation is not accorded to them. In the words of one expatriate manager in Champion:

> Before Bankole came to power, things were usually quiet on the workers' side. The leader before him was a sensible fellow and rarely created any problems. But with Bankole from the start it was clear that there would be trouble. Before, there was no real threat of strike action, but once Bankole was elected, strikes were always on the cards.

On the whole employers have given in to such demands without much struggle, because, one suspects, the costs to them have proved relatively slight. The more important contrast with the past is that union leaders are always consulted today where there is the possibility of individual workers being sacked. In all companies, the circumstances under which employees can be dismissed are now clearly laid down, and if there is any suggestion that a worker is being ill-treated, house union leaders act quickly to defend him to the hilt. It will be evident why this is the case: after wage-levels, job security is of the greatest importance to all workers. Should it be suggested that union leaders are lax in defending their workers on this count, then their reputations are seriously affected. So this is one issue on which union leaders act with great speed and efficacy.

Above all, the new men have managed to make some progress on the issue of general wage levels and done so either by threatening strike action, or in some cases, bringing production to a halt. On coming to power in the late 1960s they pressed for general wage-increases across the board. They either demanded flat rate increases or ones on a graduated scale with the largest increases going to the lowest paid ranks of permanent employees. In some instances their initial demands were for increases as high as 25 per cent, although in most they were for rather less. Invariably these demands were rejected outright by employers, and were followed by negotiations lasting several days or weeks. These negotiations also included discussion of wide ranging issues which made them complex affairs. Of these developments we shall have more to say below. Here it is sufficient to note that the house unions have had some degree of success: the new men gained upward revisions in the wage-levels of their members, a development which in most factories established a major precedent for the future.

The Limitations on House Unionism

To summarize the preceding account, in the space of only six years, the workers' circumstances *vis-à-vis* employers have been greatly transformed. Before 1964 there were no house unions, job insecurity was endemic, and wages were at the minimum level for the vast majority of workers. The first major change occurred when the General Strike raised the major barriers to combination, and at least the organizations were established even if incumbent leaders were conservative. Of subsequent developments one might say that the new leaders, in conjunction with members anxious to improve their shared conditions, have allowed much of the potential of the house union system to be realized.

The close relationship between leaders and followers which the house union system allows, has throughout been crucial in allowing workers to advance their shared interests. The General Strike created a situation which could be quickly capitalized upon by individuals prepared to take the lead in getting the unions underway. Once these proved unsuitable, then they were removed with relative ease and replaced by men considered more appropriate on the shopfloor. By virtue of their proximity to the members, the new men were able to quickly gear their organizations to advancing the workers' collective interests. Having created a sense of confidence in their leadership, such men as Akanale and Bankole have been able to take advantage of the physical concentration of the workers and their readiness to fight for subsequent improvements. In brief, as a response to local level exigencies, the house union system has considerable organizational merits which are now being well explored. On the other hand, the system has its in-built weakness. Whilst it has proved relatively successful in relation to employers at the local level, it is not a system which is easily transformed into an organizational force in relation to the government. At this point, a digression is required.

So far in this chapter, as indeed throughout the book, I have been writing in the present tense as a matter of convenience. But this is very much a study tied in time: I have been describing the workers' social organization and socio-economic circumstances in Agege and Ikeja in 1970 and 1971. As indicated in Chapter 1, this was a period of substantial economic and political change in Nigeria, coinciding as it did with the months following the end of the civil war and the attempts of the military government to lay the basis for post-war reconstruction. Most of the aspects of social organization discussed so far can be analytically separated out from these wider political developments. Migrants' social networks or occupational rank in the factories, for example, are not much affected by such developments. This is not the case with the unfolding of the Ikeja house union movement by 1970 and 1971. At this point in the analysis it becomes essential to refer to developments in the wider political environment both before 1970 and at the time of my fieldwork.

The Federal Military Government pursued the war effort against Biafra from 1967 to 1970. This affected the house unions on two main counts. The first was that, in order to facilitate the war effort, an ordinance was passed forbidding strike action or engaging in any form of incitement to strike. Thus it was in existence at the time the new men in the unions came to power. It was also renewed in both 1970 and 1971 so that throughout the period I am describing, strike action was illegal. Not surprisingly, house union leaders and workers were much concerned about this. It was popularly referred to as Decree 53, and we shall come back to it several times in this chapter and the next.

The other major influence of this period was that of inflation. During the war years the military government paid little attention to this, but it was of quite critical importance for the house unions from about 1967 onwards. It was not an entirely new development.

Since 1964 when the government-stipulated minimum wage-rate was last changed, inflation in the Lagos metropolitan area had risen steadily, but it was in the years 1967 to 1970 that inflation reached new and remarkably high levels. It is difficult to be specific about the effects of this on the real wages of the workers in the European companies. Official statistics are notoriously inadequate for the Lagos metropolitan area, and because of the continuous regrading going on in the factories it is difficult to compare like jobs with like. However, the costs of accommodation and foodstuffs had, from 1967 onwards, increased at rates of between 10 per cent and 15 per cent per annum so that substantial wage increases were necessary to keep wages in step with rising costs of living.[8]

Turning back to the unions, both factors, inflation and Decree 53, considerably influenced the later years of their development and the nature of leadership provided by the new men. Immediately the rate of inflation became of considerable consequence. They introduced it as an issue of prime concern into the first wage negotiations which they instigated, for some in 1967, for others in 1968. Accordingly their initial wage claims were frequently of the order of 15 per cent to 25 per cent although in the event, these claims were scaled down in the course of bargaining. Most initial wage claims resulted in increases of between 8 per cent and 13 per cent. At this juncture I should acknowledge that I do not know how these particular figures were reached. Discussions with employers and union leaders as well as reading transcripts of negotiations tended, on the whole, to be unenlightening. I suspect in fact that one cannot establish any clear pattern: the range of factors involved was probably such as to ensure that the final figures were somewhat arbitrary. Nor can I adequately explain why in some firms the threat of strike action was transformed into collective action whilst in others it was not. Again I suspect that a number of influences led to this being somewhat random.

Two major developments, however, arose out of successive annual wage negotiations in the late 1960s. The first was that in the light of Decree 53 the ability of the house union leaders to press up to the hilt for wage increases was severely restricted. Lengthy strikes were not possible since these would attract the interest of the government. Where short strikes of only a few days duration were embarked upon, then this appeared not to be the case, but it was clear that the illegality of strike action was a factor which employers could exploit. The other development was that whilst European employers were evidently prepared to grant some increase in wage-levels, in return for agreement to measures which would increase factory productivity, there was no question of their granting annual increases which would keep wages in line with increases in the overall cost of living. As leaders entered their second or third annual bargaining sessions, and as inflation increased, it became very evident that expatriate employers were intending to draw a firm line on any suggestion that wage increases should match rises in the cost of living. This was not their responsibility but the government's. Moreover, employers argued, not only had their profitability declined during the civil war, the military government was effecting major changes in import policy, changes which in many cases resulted in their own commodity prices being undercut.[9]

This brings us to the major subject of concern to both union leaders and followers alike. By the time my fieldwork began in 1970 it was clear to all that the Ikeja house unions had reached a critical stage in their development. At the local level in relation to employers, they had become viable organizations which had successfully earned the right to consultation, established job security and gained wage increases. With the exception of the last, these achievements and others did not have to be repeated. The only outstanding and recurrent issue was that of wage-levels, but it was precisely on this issue that the existing system now appeared inadequate to the demands and interests of union members at large. It was now essential for the unions to develop some political clout. As far as union leaders and workers were concerned, it was only through effective and sustained political action that (i) general wage increases could be won, (ii) other measures might be forthcoming from the government in order to combat the worst effects of inflation (price fixing, for example), and (iii) Decree 53 might be repealed in order that, at the local level, there could be a return to free collective bargaining between employers and workers. In a nutshell, by 1970 it appeared that the house union system had reached its limits of development. Over the years this system had proved effective in response to local level exigencies. Most of the gains made were a reflection of the extent of that adaptability, but by 1970 it was unequal to the influence of external factors as these affected the local situation. There was, however, rather more to the situation than this. When I discussed the current situation with leaders and workers, most had a quite clear idea as to what might be done in the light of these developments, but there was no move afoot to put such diagnoses into practice. The result was that despite the considerable political potential of the workers they considered themselves relatively powerless in relation to government, a feeling which compounded their sense of grievance and disenchantment with their status in the modern urban industrial setting.

To elaborate, in the course of discussion, union presidents and members widely argued that there were two options open to them. The first of these was for the individual house unions to throw their weight behind one of the more prominent labour congresses in Nigeria, the United Labour Congress (U.L.C.), or the Nigerian Trade Union Congress (N.T.U.C.), both organizations with some influence at the national level. However, it must be emphasized that they were not especially effective political organizations mainly because of the limited nature of their affiliated memberships which in total represented only a small proportion of the Nigerian working class, and their consequent financial dependence on subsidies from competing international organizations. For these reasons they could, for the most part, be ignored by the government in power. Ikeja leaders and ordinary workers frequently argued to me that were their own house unions to become attached to the U.L.C. or N.T.U.C. then this would give such bodies considerable strength, which is undoubtedly accurate. Furthermore they argued that, following their affiliation, other unions in the Lagos area would follow their lead, for one of the problems facing such bodies was that their slight degree of effectiveness was in itself an obstacle to recruiting new members.

The second possibility, also widely countenanced, was that of developing at Ikeja some form of over-arching organization which could represent the Estate labour force to the government. That is, leaders and followers considered it at least a possibility that individual house unions could pool their collective resources and that a core group of union presidents could be elected to present their case to those in power.

In other words, union leaders and workers were well aware of their considerable collective political potential. On the Estate was concentrated the largest single body of privately employed wage-earners in the country. They were also, comparatively speaking, the most organized body of workers in Nigeria, and, as will become clear in Chapter 6, under particular circumstances they could act effectively in relation to government. Yet, notwithstanding general awareness of these possibilities, neither of these options were being taken up in 1970. The Ikeja unions continued to maintain their distance from the U.L.C. and the N.T.U.C., nor was there any move afoot for the house unions to co-operate together with a view to forming an Ikeja labour council, and, therefore, some degree of organizational unity. It is of course with some trepidation that one asks why some social form does not occur in a particular context, as it involves raising a hypothetical possibility which cannot be empirically validated. Yet I hope it is now clear that it is worth considering why the house unions did not exercise either of these options. The ramifications of their not doing so were clearly considerable: without any representation in the corridors of political power the house unions faced considerable restrictions on their degree of effectiveness at the time, and in the future.

The Politics of House Unionism

There are two main reasons why these options have not been taken up. These are the workers' generalized antipathy towards any kind of leadership distanced from them, and the manner in which the style of leadership provided by union presidents reinforces rather than mitigates the existing highly segmented form of the Ikeja labour movement.

As regards the first, there is, amongst the Ikeja workers, a fundamental cynicism concerning all things political. This is so great as to present a major barrier to any wider form of worker combination. One recurrent comment amongst the Ikeja workers, and one which indicates their affinity for their house union leaders, is: 'The only leader to be trusted is the leader working at your side'. Workers share the view that any form of leadership and representation not immediately open to their inspection and sanctioning will operate to the benefit of leaders alone and not to those whom they purport to represent. It is difficult to capture the workers' cynicism concerning figures who are removed from them. But it warrants emphasis that it is a product of bitter experience and not mere conservatism or cultural inertia. It is a response to previous situations, most especially within their places of origin, where relatively powerless lower class groupings have had their interests endlessly exploited and manipulated by politicians and their aides. This is not the place to review the recent history of party politics in Nigeria, but, as is well known, it has been characterized by ethnic rivalries, nepotism, corruption and considerable violence, in brief the consistent abuse of power. It is in reflection of these experiences that workers have come to view with a jaundiced and suspicious eye any form of leadership which is not immediately accessible to them. Thus, whilst in the course of discussion, workers indicated to me the gains which might follow from having some measure of representation towards the government, they invariably added that their leaders would misappropriate funds, be easily bought off, or would simply collapse in the face of opposition from the political class, thus leaving themselves in much the same unrepresented situation as currently obtains.

Of greater consequence than such prevalent sentiments is that the nature of leadership by house union presidents is such as to perpetuate and reinforce the autonomy of their unions from one another and from existing national labour congresses. Obviously in the light of previous analysis, the formation of any overarching Ikeja based representative grouping, would require the initiative and indeed leadership of present day union presidents. Both developments would require some lessening of the high degree of autonomy of the house unions. Now, by contrast with labour movements elsewhere in urban Africa, one of the important features of the Ikeja house union system is that all elected officers are unpaid. The only material gains are those won for the labour force as a whole. Yet the prestige attached to union presidencies is considerable, the more so since in Agege there are no formal organizations of comparable size which wage-earners might lead. As a result, union leadership by its very nature, allows energetic and ambitious men who value prestige and power virtually the only institutionalized roles from which they can realize these. To be a union leader is to occupy a coveted position, and accordingly presidents are engaged in tactics which consolidate their power base. This in its turn means that they would be most loathe to surrender any degree of their control to others, as would be required for any form of higher political representation to develop.

There are several distinctive tactics whereby union presidents personalize their offices: the first is the selective assembly of a small coterie of workers drawn from both within the union executive and beyond it. On such small groups of close supporters, union presidents rely heavily for support and advice. In effect, each president has a small team inside the factory which is integral to his control of ongoing affairs within the factory. While all union executive posts are filled by popular vote, by no means all play an equal part in the running of their unions. The division of labour greatly depends on the direction and inclination of the union president, so that each delegates to those whom he wishes to favour, and with these he shares the exercise of power and prestige of leadership. Union presidents' teams also include close allies and aides drawn from the shopfloor. Most make a point of drawing close to them popular and outspoken workers from a range of different departments and sections. They are able to inform the president of prevalent opinions and specific grievances. Conversely when directed to do so, or acting on their own account, they can counter gossip about their leaders when it proves necessary. A particularly important element of this strategy is for presidents to include in their teams workers drawn from the notorious trouble spots of their factories. Not only is it from these that presidents can expect to encounter criticism directed at themselves, but they can instigate wildcat action within them when it is politically opportune to do so.

Presidents also consolidate their positions by the skillful handling of the democratic process. As noted earlier house unions are generally run in an open fashion, but union leaders are able to turn these democratic features to their distinct advantage. For example, general meetings have an aspect of stage-management about them. Presidents call meetings when it suits them to do so. The manner in which agenda items are negotiated is entirely in their hands. Furthermore, whilst it rarely happens that presidents stem dissenting opinions by invoking constitutional procedures and debating rules, it is relatively easy for them to arrive at voting decisions which they themselves most favour.[10] By having close supporters present at a meeting, a union leader can generally ensure that the right proposals receive an airing at the right time. This is by no means to suggest that majority opinion is ignored or stilled if it is not consistent with a leader's views. Presidents frequently allow opinions to emerge from the floor of meetings before elaborating their own. That these eventually prevail is quite as much a reflection of workers' confidence in present-day leaders as of the latters' stage-managing talents.

This relates to the third strategy, a particularly important one. Union presidents are able to present to their followers, in either formal or informal settings, their own particular constructions as to what has occurred in closed negotiation sessions with management representatives. In accordance with their commitment to a democratic style of leadership, presidents frequently cast themselves in the role of information broker between managements on the one hand and workers on the other. Precisely because negotiation sessions are restricted to a select few, they allow presidents a good deal of latitude in tailoring accounts as to the developments within them. Whether on major or minor issues, union leaders are accompanied to negotiation sessions by only three or four executive members, those men on whom they know they can rely for full support. Subsequently, they can place a particular gloss on the content of meetings without the possibility of these being refuted by knowledgeable others. Moreover during the course of negotiations, a host of competing issues become raised, many of which require some special knowledge, and so points of difference between leaders' policies and majority opinion on the shopfloor can be easily obfuscated. Perhaps the main advantage which accrues to presidents from the restricted nature of negotiations is that it provides them with a splendid opportunity to engage in extreme political rhetoric. On the shopfloor, in the factory compounds, as well as in general meetings, managements can be accused of delaying tactics, complicating elementary issues, attempting bribery of executive members, or hiding behind the skirts of government. These are recurrent themes as are the claims of presidents to be consistently militant and steadfast. Whilst it is doubtless true that followers are somewhat sceptical of their leaders' more grandiose claims, much of this rhetoric finds acceptance since it reinforces the major dimensions of the workers' sense of class consciousness.

In the above respects, the performances of the Ikeja unionists are little different from those of labour leaders elsewhere in urban Africa or in modern industrial societies. Tactics such as these are the stuff of day to day trade union politics. They are requirements built into the structured role of leadership. In relation to the Ikeja context they can be looked upon in two different ways. On the one hand they help explain further why house union leaders have proved successful. They are, as one would expect them to be, politically astute men who are well-attuned to the circumstances in which they are operating. By the use of personal teams, by manipulating the democratic process, and by taking full advantage of the restricted nature of industrial negotiation, they have managed, within the framework of the house union system, to realize those gains which their followers value in a relatively short period of time.

On the other hand, it is equally the case that these same strategies of leadership are the means whereby union presidents personalize their offices, and by doing so they obviate the possibility of either the house unions acting in concert in the form of an Estate-wide labour council, or throwing their weight behind existing labour congresses. Both lines of action would require presidents to give up some degree of the personal control which they are currently most concerned to extend further. A general council of Ikeja unions organized for wider political representation would require presidents to develop common policies of action which would inevitably run counter to their personal control. Furthermore, those not elected as spokesmen to, for example, the Ministry of Labour, would suffer diminished prestige in the eyes of their followers. Likewise, were individual unions to be affiliated with one of the country's existing labour congresses, presidents would have to forgo some of their authority. They would be forced publicly to concede that certain courses of action were being instigated by national figures at a considerable distance from the shopfloor, a development which would immediately raise the suspicions of those workers who have elected them into office. In short, the individual interests of union leaders and the distrust of workers for leaders beyond their immediate orbit, strongly reinforce one another.

From time to time the leaders of the country's national labour congresses make concerted efforts to recruit the well organized Ikeja unions into their ranks. They do so by making available to union presidents certain resources which are of some value to the latter, the most important being that the U.L.C., a labour congress affiliated to the Washington-based AFL-CIO, has extensive training facilities in Lagos, in particular short courses for trade unionists engaged in grass-roots organization. By sending individual members of his team on such courses, a union president can further buttress his degree of control, and make more effective the position of his union *vis-à-vis* the expatriate management. The difficulty in taking advantage of this facility is that the U.L.C. expects the house union to become a congress affiliate in return. Once again, union presidents employ their political skills to avoid such a threat to their autonomy.

To give but one brief example, in 1970 Akanale, the leader of the International house union, sent a couple of his closest followers on a short training course under U.L.C. auspices. In return the U.L.C. leaders attempted to draw the house union into its ranks. To this Akanale was adamantly opposed, and this he was to make perfectly clear at the union's annual general meeting to which the congress vice president was invited as one of several guests of honour. As is customary, the official was invited to speak. He did so, briefly, on the need for worker unity and then, at much greater length, on the U.L.C.'s intention to construct at substantial cost a new administrative centre in the capital. He produced an artist's sketch and explained, somewhat blithely, how this new building would rival those of labour movements in advanced societies, some of which he had visited. He concluded with a passionate appeal for donations. Earlier speeches had been generously received, but this was accorded only a short, polite round of hand clapping. Then Akanale rose to his feet and thanked the official for his attendance. But he went on to say that 'my workers' would be far more impressed by less emphasis on prestige projects 'like the old politicians wanted'. It was a great pity, he continued, that the only time the 'Lagos Big Guns' visited the Estate was 'when they were looking for money, but not in our hours of need'. He then quickly moved on to the next speaker as cries of 'Hear, hear!' from the floor filled the room. In a couple of sentences the union president had drawn attention to the gulf between himself and his followers on the one hand, and the distant national labour figures on the other, in addition to emphatically establishing that he intended to brook no external involvement in the affairs of his union.

Conclusion

In the first half of the chapter the major concern was to indicate certain key aspects of the organization of Ikeja trade unionism and to indicate some of the achievements of the house unions in the course of their relatively short histories. The workers are led by popular shopfloor men who have come to prominence relatively recently, and the unions which they lead are democratic institutions in which ordinary members have considerable opportunities to make themselves heard. Because of the proximity of leaders and followers, the former have been able to mobilize the latter in such a way that they have become relatively effective in relation to their expatriate employers. They have put some tangible results into their followers' hands. In other words, the workers' sense of opposition to their employers, the class consciousness which we described in the previous chapter, has been progressively channelled into institutionalized and rewarding forms of opposition at the local level. No longer are the workers faced with the exceptional job insecurity of earlier years, nor can their expatriate employers ride roughshod over their collective interests. Through their house unions they have some degree of established representation within their places of employment, including the right to enter into negotiations over prevailing wage levels.

In the second part of the chapter I found it necessary to refer, albeit somewhat briefly, to changes in the wider political environment which, by the time of my fieldwork, had come to prove especially pressing for the Ikeja wage-earners. In particular, rapid rises in the cost of living and restrictions on collective action had made it clear to union leaders and their members alike that gaining some form of representation in relation to employers was no longer sufficient to improve their shared social and economic circumstances. Whilst certain wage gains could be realized by bringing pressure to bear on their employers, it appeared increasingly unlikely that such pressure could keep wages in step with inflation in the metropolitan urban area. Briefly, one might suggest that from the inception of the house union system as a response to the compartmentalized nature of manufacturing on the Estate, there has been a measure of built-in redundancy to that system. It was inevitable that eventually the Ikeja trade union movement would have to turn to representing the workers' collective interests to the national government. This development had emerged by 1970. But as I have tried to show in the latter part of the chapter, whilst the requirement of wider political representation was widely appreciated, and whilst too there were certain options open to union leaders and their members, these were not attractive or viable courses of action.

So this account of this segmented Ikeja trade union movement catches the house unions at an important watershed in the course of their development. The constituent elements of the movement are faced with the problem common to any attempt at worker combination in a capitalist setting where, in the last analysis, the power of government is paramount to local level relationships between employers and employees. This is the difficulty of being transformed from organizations initially geared to the industrial framework into a movement oriented to winning influence within the supra-local political arena. The workers and their leaders have to set aside the industrial concerns of the past and increasingly turn to political concerns of the present and future. No doubt this will happen, and perhaps relatively soon. This however is to move in the direction of speculation. Our concern here is rather to stress, in conclusion, that having reached this difficult watershed stage, the workers are especially aware of the enormous part played by the government in the determination of their life-styles and life-chances. Without intervention on the part of government, even the ephemeral periods in which recent migrants enjoy some material benefit from wage-employment seem destined to disappear, as a larger proportion of their wages is taken up in purchasing bare necessities. Amongst more established workers, the rising costs of living seem likely to consume even those slight sums of money which might be set aside for self-employment. Finally, notwithstanding the efforts which they have made to build up the efficacy of their house unions, much of this investment appears to have been in vain, since circumstances beyond the Estate have overtaken the possibilities for adaptive response within it.

In the next chapter we will describe how, in late 1970, the military government took action with a view to ameliorating the conditions of Nigerian workers on low fixed incomes. It should be emphasized that this was not in response to representation by the workers, and of this those at Ikeja were well aware. Under more normal circumstances, workers consider themselves relatively powerless to influence government decision making, and so their collective resources are primarily concentrated on keeping up the pressure on their employers. Whilst to do so has its limits of effectiveness, any degree of improvement in their wage levels is welcome under the circumstances.

6 Workers, Unions and Rebellion

In this final chapter my main concern is to describe the political status of the Ikeja workers in relation to the wider political environment of Nigerian society. I do so by reference to the major industrial and political disputes which occurred in early 1971. First, a brief overview of some points arising from earlier chapters is in order.

It will be evident by now that, while the Ikeja factory workers are relatively recent members of the modern urban industrial milieu, they are nevertheless wage-earners who have developed an extensive and effective range of organizational responses to the pressures of industrial employment.[1] For those on the shopfloor, their involvement in trade unionism is of an unqualified nature since their individual circumstances are integrally linked to the internal organization of the house unions, the effectiveness of their leaders, and the readiness of their fellows to act collectively in protection of shared interests. That they are, above all other considerations, wage-earners is indicated by their sharing a proletarian culture which is constantly drawn and elaborated upon at Ikeja and in the Town. This cultural system highlights the distinctive nature of the workers' relationships to the means of industrial production and the incompatibility of their interests with those of their employers. It also provides the workers with a constant source of legitimation for their collective actions and more generally helps them make sense of the diverse sets of relationships in which they are involved on the Estate.

This is similarly the case with respect to their relationships within the social setting of Agege town. The workers themselves are very much aware that the nature of their interpersonal relations is largely

139

determined by their low rates of pay and job insecurity. From a sociological perspective too, it has proved necessary to relate these aspects of their class position to the form and content of their interaction with brothers and other members of the urban community. As factory employees are the focus of this study, I have not described the social organization of the Town's non-wage-earning population. It should be stressed though, that their relations are often of a different order to those of the factory workers.[2] Be that as it may, the latter are full members of this thriving commercial community. They are social actors in two radically different social worlds and it is in their involvement in both of these that one finds the roots of their disenchantment.

The Workers in Political Perspective

This discontent is further compounded by the enormous divide which exists between the workers' shared circumstances and the lifestyles and life-chances of Nigeria's national bourgeoisie which is particularly concentrated in the capital. These privileged members of the population are generally found in several distinct residential enclaves of metropolitan Lagos, for example Ikoyi Island, Maryland Estate, Palm Grove Estate and the Ikeja Government Residential Area, all of which are cut off from surrounding low-class locations by roads, public buildings, railways and barbed wire fences.[3] Within these superior residential areas, mansions, expensive bungalows and costly modern flats abound. Within them too are concentrated such government-financed services as decent roads, water and electricity supplies, and hospitals which in Mushin, Ajegunle, or Agege itself are few and far between. Furthermore, the residents of these enclaves possess many of the trappings of personal wealth, ranging from Mercedes cars, imported furniture and domestic appliances, to the best in traditional and Western-style clothing.

In these circumstances it is scarcely surprising that in the course of day to day life the Ikeja workers frequently articulate a marked sense of resentment against the prosperity of the few by comparison with their own relatively poverty stricken circumstances. Likewise it is to be expected that at times of industrial and political conflict, the manifest injustice of these gross material inequalities becomes one of the major grounds on which workers justify a challenge to the authority of those in government circles. The major source of their grievance, however, is the extent to which successive civilian and military governments have reinforced the divisions between rich and poor. The general impression is that the role of government is to give more to those who have wealth, comfort and privilege, at the direct expense of those who lack all such scarce resources. As we shall see, these constantly articulated grievances become inextricably bound up with particular ones arising out of specific government actions.

Such critical judgements of wider inequalities are by no means the preserve of the Ikeja factory workers. Indeed, a number of recent studies have indicated a generalized antipathy among the poorer classes of Nigerian society to its unequal structure. This antipathy was central to the *agbekoya* movement in western Nigeria's cocoa-belt, a peasant rebellion which in 1968 and 1969 proved equal to the military government's repeated attempts at containment and repression.[4] Discontent with wider inequalities has also been reported as pervasive amongst Hausa factory workers in the northern city of Kano,[5] and research in several southern Nigerian urban centres, especially in the city of Ibadan, has detailed the disenchantment prevalent amongst the self-employed urban poor and the unemployed.[6]

Hostility towards the political order is quite as widespread amongst the self-employed who comprise the majority of townspeople in Agege. Among the factory workers' fellow townsmen, the tailors, small traders, blacksmiths, motor mechanics, drivers and carpenters, one continually encounters highly unfavourable assessments of the extreme concentration of wealth and power in the hands of a privileged minority. Like the workers, the self-employed stress that such wealth has frequently been acquired by dubious means. They feel that whilst inequality between men is in the natural order of things, it is not proper for this minority to have annual incomes thirty, forty or more times greater than the mass of the population at large. Above all, the self-employed are unequivocally hostile to the way in which government resources invariably seem to be channelled in the direction of the already prosperous instead of alleviating the difficulties of the labouring poor.

We will return to these issues in conclusion. Yet it should be emphasized that, while the social and economic organization of Agege's self-employed population is such as to militate against the transformation of their sentiments into concerted action, this is not the case, even on *a priori* grounds, with the factory workers. For the most part, the self-employed are involved in extreme competition among themselves for regular custom and a network of steady clients. Alternatively, they are dependent on the patronage of well to do urban entrepreneurs and Big Men in Agege. These factors, and others, create and reinforce divisions within their ranks. The ideology of entrepreneurship further stresses the ideals of self-help, the need to continually strive on an individual basis to overcome the many obstacles placed in the way of efforts to get on in the world. By contrast, the factory employees would appear to be inclined towards collective political action, despite the limitations of the formal house union system outlined in the previous chapter. They are physically concentrated at work in a manner in which the self-employed are not, they have experience of concerted action under respected leaders of their own choosing, their ideology is such as to encourage and legitimate protest against those whom they consider to exploit them, and since their basic wage rates are directly tied to decision-making in government circles, so their awareness of the degree to which their circumstances are related to the actions of those in power is all the more heightened. The specific point to which we will return is that by engaging in action which questions the wider political order, the workers express a sense of hostility which is widespread and do so on behalf of other underprivileged members of the urban population who do not have the same organizational capacity as themselves. So whilst we are now concerned with the relationship of the factory workers to the government, we must bear in mind that in the Town the workers share with the self-employed both poverty-stricken circumstances and a pervasive resentment against the structure of the society at large.

The Dimensions of Political Status

There are, in my view, some general requirements which must be met in any attempt to describe the political status of an underprivileged group. The first of these is that an analysis must be grounded in particular events and social situations. Only from sequences of collective action is it possible to identify and extrapolate those shared interests and sentiments which encourage members of a subordinate population to oppose the prevailing political order. To put it another way, an assembly of non-contextual statements by a given population provides little guide as to how they may order their activities in concert. No doubt to many readers the point will seem trite, but it is necessary to make it here since the formal interview technique, despite its many and widely-recognized limitations, is increasingly being used to describe the political consciousness of the urban poor and their perceptions of government.[7] The present writer takes his position from F.G. Bailey: 'Crisis calls for action and action is a surer basis than talk on which to found a sociological analysis'.[8]

The next analytical requirement is that the political status of a class, or a segment of it, must be related to the wider class system.[9] A class as such only exists in relation to other classes, and since these are relationships of power, any analysis should make reference to patterns of class consensus and conflict around the State where the bulk of available scarce resources is concentrated. In short, key issues which must inform attempts at class analysis in Africa are: who controls the State and how are its resources deployed? It does not however seem to me necessary to present a complete class analysis, rather it is sufficient to merely sketch in those elements of the wider system which bear directly on the class population under detailed consideration.

The third requirement is that the political importance of a class at any particular moment in time must be informed by an appropriate historical perspective. In order to properly assess the present political standing of a subordinate population, one needs to have a notion from whence it has come. This requirement is quite as applicable to the study of a small local level population as it is to a much broader one. In that the political importance of a composite class population is in part a product of its component elements or segments, then small populations quite as much as substantial ones have to be evaluated within their respective trajectories of change.

I hasten to add that these are ideal concerns rather than ones which will be met below. The second point implicitly concedes the need for a political economy of Nigerian society, and therefore a study of a quite different order to the present one.[10] The third acknowledges that it is the social historian rather than the social anthropologist who can properly evaluate the changing political status of a working class population. (It is by no means irrelevant to note that the seminal anthropological study of the political processes surrounding the emergence of an African wage-earning population, A.L. Epstein's *Politics in an Urban African Community*, is one which has a most powerful historical dimension to it.) Since the Ikeja labour forces are only very recently-formed, a description of their present political significance by contrast with the past can only be informed by a shallow historical perspective. Moreover, it would be easy to overstate their importance by virtue of concentrating on them, so it is appropriate to stress that the Ikeja labour force is (even if the largest) only one concentration of factory workers in Nigeria, and that the privately-employed labour force in the country is small by contrast with the majority of those in the employment of the State.

Having made these somewhat negative points, we can set against them rather more positive ones. The first is that quite fortuitously during my fieldwork, the Ikeja workers were involved for over three weeks in a major conflict with the expatriate employers and the military government. Second, the interests and sentiments which informed the workers' collective rebellion emerged with considerable clarity and showed how they conceptualize their structured relationship to their political rulers. Third, in that there were strong similarities between the circumstances of 1971 and those of the 1964 General Strike, it is possible to indicate the changing political status of the labour force over the space of some six years. Lastly, the general point I wish to make is the modest one that the events of 1971 constituted a concerted opposition to the government by the Nigerian working class in private employment which adds to the tradition of opposition which has so far been the preserve of the majority of wage-earners in the employment of the State. In brief: what is now the relationship of the workers to those in power, how has this changed over the years, and what is their collective status in broader historical perspective? To answer these questions we need initially to outline the distribution of power in Nigerian society and the position of the workers in this unequal system of relationships.

The Wider Political Framework

In contemporary Nigeria, exceptional power is concentrated in the hands of a small dominant political class. Over the space of some ten to fifteen years, a number of senior politicians and leading bureaucrats have emerged to control national decision-making offices from which they are able to direct the course of economic and political development in Nigeria. As such their decisions have major effects on the life-styles and life-chances of the majority of Nigerian citizens who have been fully incorporated into the wider market system. The common characteristic of these politicians and bureaucrats is that they have maintained fairly continuous control over the major resources of the State. Many of the former have been prominent throughout Nigeria's recent political history. Although recurrent political crises have ensured the temporary removal of some, the survivors have demonstrated a remarkable capacity to ride out periodic changes in governments ostensibly in power. The ability of the latter to maintain a relatively low political profile has allowed them a more persistent degree of control over decision-making offices. Permanent secretaries, chairmen of marketing boards and the heads of planning and economic development agencies have rotated between various positions of power, and this has buttressed their degree of personal influence and control rather than diminished it. Their experience and expertise in particular have rendered them indispensable to senior military figures within the political class, for not only do the military lack the training and skills to direct national economic and administrative changes, but there has been a rapid turnover in the military leadership as a result of *coups d'état*, the course of the civil war, and differences within senior military ranks.[11] The political class then is a composite group of military leaders, political figures and prominent bureaucrats, but it is the last two mentioned who have had the most lasting impact on the direction of change in the society as a whole, and continue to do so.

By virtue of their control of scarce resources concentrated within the State, the political class has been able to compound its power base by promoting the interests of prominent sections of Nigeria's national bourgeoisie. The dominant characteristic of this section of the population is its wealth and prestige. In sociological terms, it is best described as a status category in that its members share an affluent life-style which clearly distinguishes them from the population as a whole. It is not an economic class in the strict Marxist sense since only segments of this bourgeoisie own or control the varied means of production in Nigeria or, alternatively, dominate noteworthy spheres of the market economy. Occupationally it is a diverse social category which includes leading bureaucrats, indigenous and expatriate industrial managers, indigenous businessmen, higher ranking military officers, plus an extensive range of salaried professionals including doctors, lawyers, and academics. Though somewhat concentrated in Lagos and Ibadan, they are widely distributed throughout the major urban areas, and they are an ethnically mixed population. Notwithstanding this diversity, most of them, and particularly those gathered together into representative organizations, are valuable allies to the political class since in a variety of local contexts they exercise power over substantial sections of the country's grass-roots population.

The relationships between the political class and varied segments of the bourgeoisie are, however, by no means stable and constant over lengthy periods of time. On the contrary, many of the major changes in Nigerian society over the past decade derive from the political class redistributing the resources of the State in order to promote (or demote) the interests of those below them. That is, the dominant class is able to sustain its paramountcy by switching its ties of allegiance according to prevailing economic and political circumstances, whether internally or externally generated. A major consequence of this is that the national bourgeoisie remains, as it has always been, a fragmented economic and political category. Notwithstanding its shared prosperity and privilege, there are many important divisions of interest within it. This is not to suggest that the power of the political class can take any direction. To some extent decision-making in the highest echelons is restricted by the prospect of alienating major segments of the bourgeoisie, and by developments in the wider international political economy. But nor is the course of economic and political development a mere reflex of that wider economy. Most especially because of the capital resources generated by oil, the political class has a good deal of autonomy in the promotion of internal development on lines required by their interests and suggested by their dominant ideologies.

This sketch map of upper echelon power relationships will be fleshed out in a moment. The point to be made at this juncture is that the socio-economic circumstances of any segment of the urban and rural poor are directly affected by changes of allegiance and alliance between the political class and others with power. Specifically, for our purposes, the conditions of wage-earners in private employment are closely related to the political influence of their expatriate employers at any particular moment in time. By 1970 and 1971, the alliance between the political class and expatriate employers was by no means as firm as it had been in earlier years. It was a relationship which was somewhat ambiguous and in the process of change. In the late 1950s and early 1960s, those in control of the State had been prepared to pay a high price to attract overseas capital into the country in order to stimulate the growth of industrial manufacturing. This had been consistent with their conception of national development which was intended to provide jobs and cheaper consumer goods, and to fulfil the image of a nation-state taking the first steps towards industrialization. This made it necessary to import capital assets and technological skills, and, as a result, expatriate industrialists enjoyed considerable political patronage as the embryonic political class devoted massive State resources to the promotion of fledgling industry. In Lagos and other major urban centres, regional and Federal governments committed themselves to providing necessary infra-structural facilities at very low costs to employers. These benefits were increased by complex long-term agreements on tax-free periods, facilities for the repatriation of profits, low-cost import duties, and many other measures.[12]

By 1970, the situation was very different. The crucial factor was oil. The revenues generated by oil appeared to have diminished financial dependence on inflows of foreign investment. Its impact had been held in check by the civil war, yet it now seemed clear that the prospects for internally-financed industrial development on a large scale were assured.[13] Other changes enhanced this prospect. One was that the intervening period had seen the rise of a prosperous class of indigenous businessmen increasingly eager to enter those spheres of industry controlled by expatriate owners and employers. There had also emerged a substantial category of university-educated professional men similarly ambitious to gain greater prominence in large-scale industry and manufacturing. The precise nature of these changes need not concern us. The general point is that by 1970 the political class was especially concerned to promote the interests of these indigenous businessmen and well-qualified professionals. By contrast, the position of expatriate employers was being viewed with a critical eye, not the least influence here being that the course of the civil war had led many Nigerians to be deeply distrustful of any foreign involvement in the country and to talk, if not act, in terms of greater self-reliance.

In short, in the uppermost echelons of Nigerian society, there was considerable fluidity in the arrangement of power relationships, and these changes were of consequence for both expatriate employers and their employees, including the Ikeja factory workers. It will be remembered that one of the difficulties facing the Ikeja house unions by 1970 was the adamant opposition of employers to the suggestion that wage-increases should match rises in the cost of living. Employers were strongly arguing that their own circumstances were difficult and in no way allowed of such increases. There were several influences at work in this, but there is no doubt that in major part it was a product of decisions within the political class to encourage greater competition in areas of the economy hitherto dominated by expatriate employers. Radical changes in import policy were increasingly affecting the sales and profitability of expatriate enterprises, and this trend seemed likely to continue according to various proposals outlined in Nigeria's second major development programme.

It is not, however, only changes in the relationship of their employers to the political class which have ramifications for industrial workers. Changes within their own ranks are equally influential. In the political framework sketched out above, I have been concerned to emphasize the relationship between the political class and the national bourgeoisie. Generally speaking these relationships have provided the major dynamic for processes of political change, whilst the interests of the mass of the population have been ignored, accorded a secondary role, or taken into account in a highly selective fashion. Yet it must be emphasized that since independence, the growth of the urban wage-earning class has been a phenomenon which no incumbent group of political rulers has been able to ignore. Whilst available statistics are inadequate, it seems possible that within the space of a decade those in wage-employment almost doubled from around 900,000 in 1960 to roughly 1.8 million in 1970. As these are concentrated in the major urban areas, and especially in Lagos, so changes in their circumstances affect large numbers of the self-employed who service them. Moreover, that the wage-earners are greatly dissatisfied with their collective lot is widely appreciated at all levels of Nigerian society. The General Strike of 1964 provided an unqualified demonstration of the impact they can make, for on this occasion they found a common issue to unite them against the government, itself the country's senior employer. Finally, throughout the 1960s, not only had the number of local level trade unions grown considerably, but there had been a continual rise in the number of recorded strikes, not to mention the undoubtedly numerous ones which failed to gain recognition in official statistics.[14]

Thus changing alliances and conflicts in the upper reaches of Nigerian society continually affect the lot of those in the lower echelons of the social system. Within the overall pattern of change the wage-earners are becoming a force on the political map which is not easily ignored. With these points in mind we can turn to the events of 1971 from which it becomes very clear that under particular circumstances, the factory workers are able to realize their considerable political potential.

The Adebo Commission and the Roots of Conflict

In the first instance, the source of conflict arose from the military government's attempt to appease those on low wages following the conclusion of the civil war. It was well recognized that considerable hardship had fallen upon the country's wage-earners; that the military government turned its attention to their conditions in itself indicated that it was inclined to accord them some political significance, despite a lack of formal representation. This acknowledgement took the form of a Wages and Salaries Review Commission whose brief was to conduct a general enquiry into the conditions of workers in the public sector. Commissions such as this had been a feature of the colonial and post-colonial periods, and on all previous occasions some increase had been recommended for the majority of workers in the employment of the State. The same increases had usually been granted to workers in the private sector though not always without their having to take strike action, and so, not surprisingly, the initiative aroused considerable interest among the Ikeja workers. A further feature of earlier commissions was that they were headed by respected men unconnected with national politics; this too proved the case in 1970. The appointed head was Chief Simeon Adebo, an ambassador to the United Nations in New York and a person who, it was widely felt, would preside in the same 'objective' spirit as his predecessors. It was announced that the Adebo Commission would from mid-1970 begin the lengthy process of gathering information from all possible quarters, and for a time it fell out of the public eye, attracting only intermittent attention from the mass media.

Towards the end of 1970, interest was much revived by an opportunist initiative on the part of a hastily-formed group of labour congress leaders who went under the grandiose title of the United Committee of Central Labour Organizations (U.C.C.L.O.). One of the group's moves was to draw up a lengthy memorandum[15] to the Adebo Commission in which, on the basis of some remarkably abstruse statistical formulations, it was claimed that the Minimum Living Wage for the average Nigerian worker with a wife and child was £N116.5s.8d. per month. This was eleven times greater than the existing minimum wage, and was revised to an 'irreducible' £N48.10s. – almost five times the minimum wage. Among the Ikeja workers this suggestion was received with considerable amusement. It was also taken to indicate the ubiquitous follies of national labour figures. Of considerably greater appeal, since it appeared more feasible, was the suggestion that, as the Commission's enquiry was to be an extended one, an interim cost of living award would be in order. This would at least allow low fixed income earners some respite against the inflation which had continued unabated since the Commission was established. Initially Chief Adebo and his colleagues set aside this notion and embarked on a tour of the twelve states. Subsequently, the major newspapers promoted the same suggestion, and it gained a widespread popularity. At this point the Commission demonstrated its sensitivity to public opinion. The tour of the states was cut short, and it presented its first report to the military government whilst stressing that several reports and further recommendations were to follow. Adebo and his colleagues clearly considered their work to have just begun.

As with the Morgan Commission of 1963 to 1964, the Adebo Commission was concerned to set its recommendations in a broad context. Several passages referred to the sacrifices which the civil war had imposed on those with low fixed incomes. This was made especially explicit in a striking paragraph which was subsequently widely quoted in the newspapers, (the emphasis is the Commission's):

Such sacrifice would be easiest to bear, however, if it was seen to fall equitably on all sections of the population such that the least sacrifice was made by those in the lowest income group. From some of the representations made to us, it is not only clear that there is intolerable suffering at the bottom of the income scale because of the rise in the cost of living, but also *that suffering is made even more intolerable by manifestations of affluence and wasteful expenditure which cannot be explained on the basis of visible and legitimate means of income.*[16]

The Ikeja workers considered this statement to sum up their own feelings precisely. Of greatest concern to them were the interim awards intended to provide some temporary relief whilst the Commission resumed its work. The report stressed that (their emphasis):

In the circumstances, the award we feel able to recommend at this time is aimed at relieving *intolerable suffering at or near the bottom of* the wage and salary levels.[17]

The principle recommendations were for increments of 1s.7d. per day for daily-paid workers and £N2 per month for wage and salary earners. It was recommended that these cost of living allowances should be paid to all workers earning less than £N500 per annum whilst those earning between £N500 and £N524 would receive increments to raise their incomes to £N524. This was the upper limit: wage-earners above this level were to receive nothing. The Commission recommended that these increases should be paid to both

State and privately-employed workers. Furthermore, all awards were to be back-dated to 1st April 1970, a period of nine months.

The government fully approved the Adebo recommendations shortly before Christmas and amongst the Ikeja workers there was a sense of jubilation. All shopfloor workers, and most others, fell well within the upper limit set by Adebo, and so it seemed they were entitled to an extra £N2 per month and backdated pay of some two months' wages; this quickly became known as 'Adebo's Christmas present'. Yet only five days after the government accorded its approval, the situation changed quite dramatically. Following a meeting with the expatriate employers' representative body, the Nigerian Employers' Consultative Association (N.E.C.A.), the Federal Commissioner for Labour announced a revision in the government's policy and a major departure from the Adebo recommendations. N.E.C.A. had argued that since some of the Association's members had allowed their employees general wage-increases since 1964, when the minimum wage-rate had last been raised, it was unreasonable to expect them to pay the same wage increments as those companies which had not done so. Chief Enahoro, the Commissioner, declared that the military government upheld this 'unjust element'. He announced that where companies in the private sector had made wage adjustments since 1964 on the basis of the cost of living, and where these adjustments were equal to or in excess of the Adebo awards, then such companies were exempted from paying the awards; where such increases had been made but were less than the awards, then companies were expected to make up the balance; where there had been no such increases in wages, the full awards had to be paid.

The Workers' Response

By any standards, the Enahoro qualification was an exceptionally clumsy political act. The decision was evidently taken on the assumption that those affected would take note of the renewal of Decree 53 banning strikes only a few months previously. Amongst the leaders of U.C.C.L.O. the response was muted; none raised a strident voice in public against the government decision. The announcement was, however, well-timed, whether intentionally or not, since it coincided with the beginning of the Christmas vacation. Factories at Ikeja were functioning with scant labour forces and most workers were travelling homewards or enjoying their vacation in the Town. Amongst the latter, expressions of astonishment and customary cynicism prevailed. In the words of one:

> We know the governments of Nigeria are filled with useless people. But look what happens here. The government gives money on one day with one hand to the workers and on the next day with the other hand takes it back again!

In the words of another, sitting in an Agege bar on the evening following Enahoro's announcement:

> Why is everyone surprised at what has happened? This is the government at work and Enahoro used to be a politician for many years, and you know what that means. Nothing goes for nothing in Nigeria.

Yet another voiced a common theme when he said:

> This is a country in which the poor have no rights at all. The government rides roughshod over us because we have no power.

A consideration which particularly rankled with the workers was the suggestion that expatriate managements had, in some benign and generous fashion, freely awarded previous wage increases to their employees. As the latter continually pointed out, they and their leaders had forced increments from their employers through the threat of strikes, and in many cases industrial action. The result was to be that 'we are victimized because the employers have managed to bribe the government men to give way on this wages business'. Thus, established stereotypes of deviousness amongst employers and of unjust and corrupt government officials came immediately to the fore. But there was widespread uncertainty amongst the workers as to how the Enahoro ruling would affect them. Most workers had no idea as to whether negotiations over the previous wage increases had involved reference to rises in the cost of living. This question could only be answered when the factories opened after the Christmas break.

Within a few days, the non-European managements on the Estate made it clear that they would pay in full the increased monthly wage and the back-dated pay. Since such firms do not allow any degree of worker representation in their factories, and therefore there had been no general wage increases within them, they had little option but to do so. Their workers were thus in the same position as the majority of State employees. In the larger European-managed companies, the situation was different. Without exception, employers considered that they came under the new government ruling since, during negotiations with house union representatives, the rising cost of living had been a factor regularly introduced into the bargaining process. The issue which now arose was the part played by the rising cost of living in influencing the size of earlier wage increases. Invariably this had been one factor amongst many others, such as new job categorizations, re-allocation of workers and the provision of canteen and medical facilities. It was therefore necessary for expatriate managements to carefully examine the details of previous wage agreements, a difficult task since records of management-union discussions are usually sketchy ones. The onus lay on European employers to demonstrate that the terms of previous agreements placed them within the Enahoro ruling, and when union leaders approached them to hear their decision, the response was that more time was needed. This was the first stage of the pattern which emerged.

While there were variations between factories, amongst union leaders and their followers a common pattern also began to unfold. The initial response was for leaders to practice democratic consultation. There was much discussion with executive members on the shopfloor. In addition, union presidents called emergency general meetings, during which several features recurred. Presidents stressed that, as far as they were concerned, their respective employers had to pay the Adebo awards in full; even though the cost of living had been invoked during previous negotiations, other issues had been far more important. Yet it was evident that managers were attempting to take advantage of the loophole which the government's change of position apparently allowed them, and as there was the likelihood of confrontation this made democratic consultation all the more necessary. As one prominent house union president declared to his followers:

> As always in this union, we the executive are only the voice of the members. As you tell us what to do, so we will do it for we are workers as yourselves. This is a democratic organization and since trouble is brewing everyone must say what he feels in his heart. Here we are all workers together and we must stand firm against the employers and the government.

The response from the workers was much the same. Whilst approving their leaders' reasoned and calculated stance, they expressed widespread hostility towards government and employers. The latter were accused of procrastination, of 'hiding behind the government's skirts', of 'cheating us of our Adebo [awards] which is our right since Chief Adebo and his men gave it to us because we are suffering'. The sharpest criticism was reserved for the military government which had, since the end of the civil war, declared its concern for the masses and promised to help them. Now it was evident that this was so much cant. One worker drew together several themes in the following fashion:

> These military men are useless just like the politicians of the old days used to be. They make promises to help the poor but they are not concerned about anything but filling their own pockets. Government and managers are just as bad. If management does not give us our Adebo then we must fight. If we allow this thing to pass by, then the managers will ignore us for ever because they will think to themselves: 'Ah! Now there is no union. The workers are weak. That is good. Then let us exploit them even more!'

In other words, general opinion was that without action the credibility of the unions would be open to question.

At the same time ordinary workers well recognized the difficulties facing their union leaders in the light of Decree 53. If union presidents formally led them out on strike, this would constitute a political act against the government and as individuals they could be held responsible for violating the ordinance: their hands were tied by the possibility of imprisonment. This being so, the workers were quite clear as to what had to be done. If action proved necessary, it would be undertaken by shopfloor men on an unofficial basis leaving union presidents to pursue a complementary strategy of maintaining formal pressure. In short, a mutual understanding was reached between leaders and followers that two avenues of response were open to them and the most effective tactic was to follow both. One worker made this explicit in the following way:

> If the management say to you that they will not pay, we the workers will know what to do. It will be up to us to act. You [he pointed to the assembled executive] can do nothing for us in this. You are no good to your wives, your children, or to us if you find yourselves in prison. Go to the management tomorrow and tell them that you can hold us back no longer. And if they still say 'No Adebo' then we will know what is necessary. When we have brought the managers to their knees, be ready to sign the papers which say that they will pay.

So action against employers and defiance of Decree 53 would be the workers' collective responsibility: the expertise of union presidents could be held in reserve for the final stage in which managements returned to the negotiating table.

For two weeks the established framework continued to hold, though it seemed unlikely to do so for long. In several factories there were occasional declines in the level of production. In all of them, union presidents repeatedly approached their employers only to be told that no decision had been reached because of factors beyond employers' control. Most employers on their own account or through N.E.C.A. had attempted to clarify their positions in relation to the Enahoro ruling. On the whole, they had come to the conclusion that the cost of living had played some part in negotiations: but was this sufficient for them to claim exemption from payment of the awards? This became the most critical issue yet despite repeated attempts to gain a ministerial ruling, none was forthcoming. Whether this was inefficiency on the part of the Ministry of Labour or deliberate inaction was unclear, but employers felt that the delay was adding to a potentially troublesome situation.

The stage of outright conflict began when, after a fortnight of rising tension, the management of a sheet-metal factory announced that it did not intend to pay. This had provoked the night-shift to begin a sit-down strike, and they were joined by the incoming early morning shift. They refused to leave the compound, whereupon the police were called in to clear the factory. This news spread like wildfire across the Estate and gave rise to several major developments. Within the next two days, the workforces of three more factories followed suit. Without awaiting statements from their employers as to whether they intended to pay the awards, shopfloor workers instigated wildcat strikes which brought production lines to a halt. The next development was that in other factories union leaders increased the pressure on their employers to the point at which some finally announced that they did not intend to pay. Following these official statements, the shopfloor workers ceased production. The composite picture to emerge was one of rapid escalation into a full scale revolt. Furthermore, shortly after the widely-reported series of disputes at Ikeja, the action spread to other concentrations of industry in Lagos, notably the Ilupeju and Apapa Industrial Estates, to other urban industrial centres in the south, and as far north as Kano.[18] It became clear that the military government, notwithstanding Decree 53 and repeated statements calling for an end to workers' illegal protests, had a major political rebellion on its hands, and one which it was apparently unable or disinclined to quell by force.

Within the arena of the Estate, the emergent strike pattern did not vary a great deal. In all the factories, the impetus came from the shopfloor, often commencing in the well-known trouble spots. This lead was taken up by other shopfloor workers in the form of go-slows which escalated into outright stoppages, with the white collar workers bringing up the rear. There was one factor which, though by no means universal, proved to be of some importance. In some firms there occurred outbreaks of violence against managers, and subsequently against military and police as they appeared on the scene. On several days in quick succession, fighting broke out as factories closed down. In the heat of the moment, unpopular managers were abused or beaten up. The usual targets were personnel managers against whom old scores were settled. The most critical situation emerged in a cocoa-processing firm where workers threatened to burn down the administration building with managers inside unless they agreed to pay the awards. What concerned employers was that the police frequently arrived too late on the scene to afford them proper protection.

Acts of violence and the possibility of further ones contributed directly to the final stage of management capitulation. Throughout these events, N.E.C.A. officials had taken the position that all employers should adhere to government policy on the award payments, a recommendation which had been reiterated as the strikes emerged. But at this later juncture a major rift emerged among certain employers. A minority seriously questioned the value of this adherence since the government appeared unready to afford them the support which they required. Proper protection of employers and their factory compounds had been slow to materialize, and the government had failed to respond to employers' requests for clarification on the Enahoro ruling. It still remained unclear as to whether the inclusion of the cost of living as a factor in previous wage negotiations entitled them to claim exemption from payment. For some expatriate managements this lack of support was symptomatic of the military government's generally equivocal attitude to European employers. Finally, and most important of all, valuable production was being lost. The result was that a handful of expatriate employers, including some from Ikeja, took the decision to break with N.E.C.A. policy, to pay the Adebo awards to their workers, and to have production resumed as quickly as possible.

With this, the combined front of employers collapsed. Two leading Ikeja firms announced their decision to pay the Adebo awards in full with disastrous consequences for other firms. Workers not yet on strike increased the pressure on their employers to announce their decision; this in turn led to their capitulation, or strikes in their companies as well. Within those firms already closed down, employers began to waiver. After some delay most determined to follow the lead of the two major firms which, by now, had resumed production. A few continued to hold out, but they did not have to do so indefinitely. In the light of continuing disputes in Ikeja, Lagos and elsewhere, the military government changed its position once again. The Enahoro ruling was repealed, and all private employers were instructed to pay in full both the monthly increases and back-dated pay awards whether or not they had previously accorded wage-increments to their workers. By this time, mid-February, only a few Ikeja firms were still at a halt. With the government's announcement, full production was quickly resumed and the Estate returned to normal after almost a month of unrest.

Conflict, Rhetoric and Shared Interests

For the Ikeja workers, and no doubt for wage-earners elsewhere in the country, the events of 1971 were of much significance. For the majority of those involved, the rebellion was the first occasion on which they had been involved in a movement of outright confrontation with the government; only a minority had been participants in the General Strike of 1964. For some of the most recently employed workers, this was the first time in which they had been engaged in open dispute with their expatriate employers. But whatever their previous experience or lack of it, all workers felt a measure of considerable satisfaction and achievement. Not only had they won the Adebo awards for which they had been fighting, they had taken on the dominant alliance of government and expatriate employers which they consider to be geared to exploiting them. Moreover, they had done so in conjunction with wage-earners in the country at large. In the words of one union president at a meeting after the successful conclusion of these events:

'As we said we would do, we brought the employers to their knees. And with our brothers in the north as well as in the south, we stood firm against the government. All of us were saying "Our exploitation is too great, it must cease from now on." Now we must make sure we drive home our advantage'.

Such political rhetoric was by no means the preserve of union leaders, it was widespread amongst ordinary workers for several weeks afterwards, and we will return to it below. Our main requirement is to consider the nature of the relationships between the major actors — the political class, the employers and the workers — for it is in the nature of these that the political status of the workers is best indicated.

In the higher echelons of the political order, what is most noteworthy is the indecisive nature of the government's performance, for this was indicative of the fluidity of power relationships at the apex of the political system. By establishing the Adebo Commission in the first instance, the government was clearly indicating that the conditions of those on low-fixed incomes were a matter of concern to it. There was no necessity for the government to have embarked on this measure. It was a matter of political expediency, an attempt to build up some degree of legitimacy now that the civil war was over, and there was never much doubt that the Commission would make recommendations in favour of the workers. Yet scarcely had the awards been announced by the government than the latter switched its support, or more appropriately its patronage, to the expatriate employers represented by N.E.C.A. Subsequently however, support for the employers was distinctly unforthcoming as strikes broke out in Lagos and elsewhere. Far from deploying to the full its powers of physical coercion, the government left the employers to bear the brunt of the workers' opposition. Finally, with a view to defusing the politically charged situation which its earlier actions had created, the government came down once again in favour of the wage-earners. This further change of policy was the most expedient course to take, but it was not one forced on the government by prevailing exigencies. In the Lagos area where the rebellion had assumed greatest momentum, most leading employers had by this juncture capitulated to their employees' demands.

Considering the overwhelming power of the government and its monopoly of the resources of the State, this equivocation and indeterminateness is in itself a reflection of the changing nature of class relationships in contemporary Nigeria. The government of the day was not prepared to back the interests of either expatriate employers or workers unequivocally in this crisis situation. As noted earlier, notwithstanding their role as representatives of overseas capital interests, the employers' political influence had declined by comparison with a decade previously. The capital resources generated from within by oil and the rise of an indigenous business class and a stratum of professionals had changed the picture, and help explain the nature of the government-employer relationship. It should be stressed that this changing political allegiance was only in the initial stages of becoming clear, but after 1970 and 1971, State support for indigenous segments of the bourgeoisie gained increasing momentum. It culminated a couple of years later in the compulsory indigenization of substantial areas of hitherto expatriate-dominated spheres of industry and manufacturing.[19] This was not a direct move against sectors of the formal economy dominated by multi-national firms, but for leading West European employers it was the thin end of the wedge, heralding a concerted thrust by those in power to redefine the position of foreign capital in the post civil war era. Thus, while our account focuses primarily on developments at the local level, these were much affected by changing class alliances at the national level.

Turning more directly to developments at the grass-roots, what do the collective actions of the Ikeja workers tell us about their own understanding of their relationship to the government? It is necessary to examine in some detail two contrasting but complementary strands which run through the workers' response: these are their concern to articulate their sense of grievance and opposition to the government, and to wrest the maximum material benefit from the situation.

The crass manner in which the government handled the Adebo awards provided a critical trigger to the collective response from below. Considering the workers' resentment against those in power, the circumstances surrounding the Enahoro ruling seemed almost designed to provoke some reaction despite the recent renewal of Decree 53. For the workers, this was a symbolically charged act. It involved the minimum wage-level which, for all wage-earners, represents most strikingly the exploitation to which they are subjected by government fiat. But the government had promised to alleviate their suffering in some way and from the Commission had received documentation of their current plight. So, as far as the workers were concerned, the government's sudden about-face could only be explained by reference to the murkiest side of power politics. It was taken as self-evident that the employers had bought off prominent political officials and/or proferred longer-term material gains to the 'Big Guns'. Here was a classic example of how alliance and intrigue between political leaders and wealthy expatriate employers operate to their mutual advantage and at the direct expense of the powerless. Despite the earlier commitment of the military leadership to dissociate itself from the excesses of pre-war civilian regimes, evidently this was so much cant and hypocrisy.

Rather more than this, the workers considered the issue to be a question of rights, as some of the above quotations indicate. This notion was employed in somewhat different ways. The more specific use referred to a right to the awards as such. In their judgement, the Adebo Commission was an independent body which had manifested the concern and objectivity of its predecessors. It was therefore only just and proper that they should receive the full awards. The other notion of rights, a use which was often indistinct and difficult to pin down, was that they considered their rights as citizens to have been transgressed. When workers used the notion in this sense, they were articulating the widespread sentiment that successive governments have treated the urban and rural poor as mere pawns, non-citizens as it were, whose very presence can be ignored when it suited those in power to do so. To this extent, the cavalier ruling on the awards was symptomatic of the persistent inclination of those in power to treat the population as if it were comprised of two camps, fully-fledged citizens — those with wealth and power, and those without full citizenship — the poor and the powerless. The government's performance, therefore, crystallized the grosser injustices of the wider political system, and provided a trigger to rebellion as well as the basis for rhetoric which declared legitimate the protest movement.

On the other hand, equally important was the pervasive strain of rational calculation and pragmatism which ran through the workers' response. At all turns of their involvement, the workers were seeking to wrest the maximum material gains from the structure of the situation with which they were faced. This pragmatism emerged in the following respects.

First, whilst the government's action was provocative, it was not one to be responded to precipitately. A full fortnight passed between the end of the Christmas break and the workers' undertaking strike action on the Estate, and what proved revealing was that workers frequently held the view that employers might decide to pay the awards anyway. That is, notwithstanding the loophole created for them by the government, it was felt that maintaining production would remain the absolute priority for Ikeja employers. There were some good grounds for this assessment of employers' circumstances. As workers are well aware, labour costs comprise a relatively limited proportion of total production costs, and small increases can be passed on to the consumer. It seemed possible then that employers would avoid running the gamut of full-scale conflicts and decide to maintain production, particularly as there was some doubt as to their ability to claim exemption from payment. It was only as time passed in early January that the possibility of this occurring seemed to be on the wane. When the first strikes broke out, general opinion had hardened that employers were delaying unnecessarily, and the least strike action could do would be to force employers into openly declaring their intention not to pay. It might even force some into quickly deciding that the costs of entering into a dispute were too high. This was the position adopted by workers in those firms which were closed down before employers declared their intention not to pay. In others the workers waited, considering that as strikes occurred elsewhere, their own companies in turn might be inclined to avoid similar disputes. It was only when this option appeared entirely closed off that shopfloor men moved into action, by which time there was nothing to be gained from holding back further.

Second, the workers' careful calculation emerged in their assessment of the situation facing the house unions and their leaders. One important consideration was not merely their immediate circumstances but future ones too. This was the issue of credibility referred to earlier. It was widely-felt, no doubt with full justification, that if there was no protest over the awards, employers would later try to press home the advantage and stand all the more intransigently against subsequent wage-claims. Yet while the future was of concern, the present was all the more so, and here the neat division of responsibilities between leaders and followers proved a most potent combination. With ordinary workers protesting on the shopfloor, union presidents were free to pursue the normal channels of representation *vis-à-vis* their employers. They were able to claim, quite rightly, that they had held back their members for as long as possible. Considering the delays on managements' side and the nature of the issues involved, they could scarcely be held responsible for the disputes which had ensued. The same division of responsibilities appears to have been effective in relation to the government. After the first week of conflict on the Estate, the Commissioner for Police in Lagos summoned to his office the half-a-dozen union leaders whose workers were by then on strike. He declared that under Decree 53 he could imprison them if he so wished, whereupon the leaders protested that this was not a situation of their making, they had tried to restrain their followers. The Commissioner repeated that this remained a possibility and instructed them to bring the workers to heel, but in the event he took no further action. It remains an open question as to why the government did not use its power, but it seems reasonable to speculate that the government was aware that this was a grass-roots protest and that the imprisonment of local level union men would have added further fuel to the flames rather than dampening them down. Be that as it may, the important point is that the calculated strategy worked out between union leaders and members proved equal to the situation.

Third, and most obvious, the workers' pragmatism was well-demonstrated by their returning to work as soon as their respective employers capitulated on the awards issue. There was no suggestion that opposition to the government should be sustained for its own sake! The task now was to keep up pressure on employers for further wage-increases at the factory level, a measured calculation which emerged particularly clearly in the sequel to the events of early 1971. It will be remembered that the Adebo Commission had announced that it planned a series of reports and policy measures which would affect the low-paid wage-earners. For some time little was heard of the Commission but when it re-emerged in November, there were several disconcerting aspects. One was that, for no apparent reason, the recommendations were presented as a final report despite the fact that several had been planned. Another was that, whilst the first report had been distinctly critical of wider inequalities, the tone of the final one appeared muted. Then again, the return to the workers was slight, only £N1 per month more, a disappointing result indeed. Finally, those who gained most were the already rich: those with salaries of between £N2000 and £N2500 were to receive increments of £N240, whilst those earning £N2500 and over were to receive £N300 per year. This seemed a truly remarkable reversal of policy considering that Chief Adebo had been concerned earlier to emphasize the *'intolerable suffering at or near the bottom of* the wage and salary levels'.

Workers' explanations for these untoward developments were quickly forthcoming: 'The government top men [i.e. senior bureaucrats] have altered the report so they will get more money'. 'Our bosses have bribed the government officials so that Adebo cannot give the workers more pay.' 'The government has told Adebo "No more reports" because he criticized the corruption amongst the Big Guns.' All this was much as to be expected. On this occasion however there was no protest from the workers. In part this was because the government handled the situation more cautiously, and all employers had to pay the small increment whatever previous wage-increases had been made within their factories. Equally though, it was a matter of the workers having reassessed their position in the light of changing circumstances. Since the initial awards had been made in January, inflation in the metropolitan area had reached a new level as traders and others increased their prices to match wage-increases. In the meantime the government had proved quite incapable of controlling rises in the cost of living. Evidently there was nothing to be gained from general wage-increases. Improvement could only come through pressure on individual managements since these increases once gained would not fuel inflation to the same extent. Moreover, workers felt that managements would be wary of provoking further industrial disputes in the light of their militancy earlier in the year.

In sum, notwithstanding the provocative nature of the government's actions and the highly charged political atmosphere which emerged, the workers' involvement was a carefully calculated one, as was the strategy to place the greatest pressure on their employers. Whilst there was abundant rhetoric in which workers expressed their hostility to the government and inequalities within Nigerian society, their concern throughout was to maximise their material gains from the crisis. With these concerns established, we can summarize their political status and the manner in which this has changed over the years.

Process and Change

The course of the Adebo affair first suggests that while the Ikeja workers are inclined towards rebellion, this latent force only comes to the surface under very particular circumstances. Rather bluntly expressed, these are workers who have to be goaded into collective action. A trigger for confrontation has to be provided from above which crystallizes their hostility to the existing system and provides the workers with a tangible rallying point for collective action. Expressed in a rather different way, these are workers who respond to situations created for them by others rather than being able to take the initiative on their own account. It is only when the government itself becomes directly and tangibly involved in policy decisions which affect their shared economic interests that the circumstances propitious for concerted opposition are created. Workers customarily feel that the government, in alliance with employers, consistently acts against their shared interests, but it is only in relation to employers that their sense of exploitation can be regularly channelled into collective action. By contrast, the tangible involvement of the government in their affairs is intermittent and undertaken on its own terms. For the most part its influence is intangible or subterranean, a feature which whilst adding to the workers' sense of powerlessness, further ensures that opposition from below can only be an occasional development.

The second proposition suggested by the 1971 conflicts is that the Ikeja workers are, so to speak, merely rebellious wage-earners. They are not, at least as yet, inclined towards issuing a fundamental challenge to the prevailing system of power and their world views are in no way influenced by millenarian ambitions. Instead their concern is the more modest goal of gaining the maximum material benefit from the existing system of relationships. They fully recognize the prevalent realities of power and, in particular, the extreme concentration of scarce resources in the hands of government. Needless to say, a major influence is that the unassailability of the present order is heightened by virtue of there being a military government in power, in conjunction with other members of the political class. The corollary of this is that they are inclined to use the entire range of resources available to them to press to the hilt their interests at the local level, for it is only at this level that headway can be made. This is not to suggest of course that political apathy is the result. Rather their incipient radicalism is compounded by a growing sense of disenchantment with any form of national leadership, and an increasing propensity to brand either civilian or military leaders with the same set of unfavourable stereotypes. But in so far as the wider political system appears unassailable, the need for well-organized house unions, led by trustworthy men drawn from the shopfloor, becomes all the more imperative and all the more the subject of concern to them. One further ethnographic point is of some relevance here. Because of the continuing nature of the enquiries by Chief Adebo throughout 1971, annual negotiations over wage-levels between employers and union leaders were suspended by common consent. Since I left the field in December 1971, I have little idea as to how the unions fared subsequently. But in the final three months of my fieldwork the annual elections of house union officers occurred in three companies which had been to the forefront of the January rebellion. Apart from some very minor changes, in all three union executives were returned intact whilst the union presidents were returned in resounding fashion. Only in one union was there an alternative candidate to the incumbent president and the latter was returned with a large majority. The other two were re-elected by common consent.

The third major generalization which can be made is that, in so far as the Ikeja workers are inclined towards opposition to rather than transformation of the status quo and require a catalyst from above in order to focus their opposition, then the upper-hand in any form of confrontation always rests with the government. Even if, for a time, the government appears to have lost control over the course of developments at the grass-roots level, nevertheless in the last analysis it has the resources on hand to re-establish that control with relative ease. Whatever their demonstrable inadequacies, those in power can defuse outbreaks of localized discontent by agreeing to the material benefits which are being demanded, an ability which they possess by virtue of the workers' pragmatism and concern with economic gain. These workers cannot afford themselves the luxury of opposition to those in power for its own sake; precisely because they have such limited resources, their collective strategy must be to glean what rewards they can from given situations. This applies quite as much to conflicts with those who control the resources of the State as it does to disputes with those who dominate the local industrial arena.

It must be acknowledged that these are very modest and somewhat negative propositions. But, as has been argued earlier, in order to maintain a proper perspective on the current political role of the workers it is necessary to do so in the light of their own past experiences and of more general trajectories of change in Nigerian society as a whole.

The situation on the Estate in 1971 may be compared to that in 1964, the year of the General Strike. The civilian government at the Federal level was passing through a severe crisis of legitimacy, and so, in an attempt to gain some measure of popularity, it responded to a call from national labour leaders to improve the conditions of low-paid wage-earners. It will be remembered from Chapter 5, however, that on receiving the recommendations of the Morgan Commission, the government equivocated over making the report public, and presenting its official reaction. Through its own political mismanagement, the government created a situation in which the appeal of the national labour leaders for a general strike was responded to throughout the country. Far from enhancing its authority, the government was severely jolted and for the first time since independence, a large section of the population openly expressed its hostility to those in power.

Consider then the changes which have occurred at Ikeja since 1964. It will be remembered that the General Strike was a critical turning point in the course of labour combination at Ikeja. Before this time there were no house unions in the factories, the workers were unorganized, open to gross exploitation, and quite without any form of representation in relation to their employers. As a result, their participation in the General Strike had three marked features. First, they joined the strike at the behest of the Joint Action Committee of national labour congress leaders: that is, they were led from outside. Second, their contribution was peripheral, not to say inconsequential, by comparison with the part played by the majority of government employees who brought the country to a standstill. Third, it was only in the aftermath of the General Strike that they acted effectively in their own right. As described in Chapter 5, they took advantage of the prevailing situation to form their own house unions, secure in the knowledge that they would not be dismissed for doing so.

In the space of only six years, therefore, the political status of the Ikeja workers has been greatly transformed. As we have seen, the Ikeja workers were to the forefront of the rebellion against the government. The dispute spread from the Estate to other factory locations in Lagos and, subsequently, elsewhere in the country. Furthermore, they were able to utilize fully their existing organizational resources to gain from the situation, and to do so with considerable political sophistication. Most important of all, the workers' actions were not set in motion by a call to opposition from beyond the local level. They were engaged in a sequence of action which was planned, co-ordinated and executed by house union leaders and the workers themselves. In brief, 1971 proved a far cry from 1964 when their political impact was negligible and their achievements were realized in the aftermath of the General Strike. This was an occasion on which they demonstrated to the government that they were by no means as powerless as they appeared. Possibly more important, they demonstrated their political potential to themselves as well. The general euphoria of the workers, following the capitulation of their employers and subsequently the government, suggested that the workers considered themselves to have come of age in the wider political arena. To this extent whilst the workers respond to situations created by others, equally it can be said, to use E.P. Thompson's phrase,[20] that these are workers who are making themselves quite as much as they are being made.

At the broader level of political change too, the 1964 General Strike is of comparative significance, although to make our central point clearly a more extended historical process must be indicated. This is that in Nigeria it has been the wage-earners in public employment who have, over several decades, performed the historical role of periodically standing in opposition to exploitation by the government in power. It is of course indisputable that the major roots of political conflict have been ethnic ones in Nigeria, and most analyses of emergent political forms have rightly concerned themselves with structured ethnic conflicts over available scarce resources. Yet having acknowledged this, it should not be forgotten that throughout the colonial period and political independence, labour forces of both a single ethnic and a multitribal composition have established a sinuous thread of class-based opposition to those in power. Hopkins has demonstrated that this tradition extends as far back as 1897 when some three thousand Lagos artisans and labourers employed by the Public Works Department came out on strike.[21] Cohen and Hughes have also detailed, for the Lagos area, numerous and varied disputes throughout the early decades of the twentieth century.[22]

Further afield, events such as the 1949 Enugu coalminers strike (which resulted in twenty-one of them being killed) indicate that wage-earners outside the capital were equally ready to transmit their sense of grievance into collective action, while the General Strike of 1945 illustrates that even during the colonial period the organizational weaknesses of the proletariat could be transcended under appropriate circumstances. Notwithstanding the ethnic basis of most structured conflict in the last decade of the colonial era, the same trend remained much in evidence, and with the General Strike of 1964, the tradition was carried over into the period of political independence. However throughout, as in the majority of ex-colonial territories, it has mainly been those in the employment of the State who have created and built upon this tradition of resistance: this historical role has long been dominated by railwaymen, port and harbour employees, labourers and construction workers, all of whom, whilst being employed by the State, have been most ready to stand in opposition to it.[23]

Thus in one major respect the rebellion of 1971 contrasted with the past for it was, of course, the rapidly growing category of workers in private employment, the factory workers, which threw its collective weight into conflict with those in power. Since the applicability of the Adebo awards to State employees was never in question, they were automatically relegated to the sidelines as the conflict took off and gained momentum. Essentially they were in the same situation as the minority of workers at Ikeja who, by virtue of being employed by non-European companies, received the awards as a matter of course. The field was left open to the predominantly unionized segment of privately-employed wage-earners to take the lead against the government. So at the wider political level, the singular feature of the sequence of events in 1971 was the political emergence of a relatively newly formed segment of the Nigerian proletariat, which up to that time had been relatively insignificant, but which henceforth would have to be accorded more importance by those in power. In the same way that the civilian government of 1964 was severely jolted by the collective action of publicly employed workers, the military government of 1971 had its authority unequivocally questioned by those in private employment. The latter for the first time made a substantial contribution to sustaining the tradition of proletarian resistance to those in power, a tradition rooted in class relationships which is all the more significant by virtue of the preponderantly ethnic basis of conflict in colonial and post-colonial Nigeria.

Conclusion

In the preceding pages I have tried to place the Ikeja factory workers in a wider sociological perspective than that allowed by the restricted boundaries of the Town and the Estate. Not only are the conflicts of early 1971 of intrinsic interest, but they have provided a convenient sequence of events with which to move from the local level to the wider political arena. The major points we have raised are that, while there is a constant fund of latent opposition to the more unequal political system, in order that this can come to the fore and be translated into collective action, an appropriate focus must be provided from within ruling circles and this must place at issue tangible and widely shared economic interests. It is only at such times that the formal organizational weaknesses of the workers can be transcended. Because of their limited economic means, the concern of these wage-earners is always to wrest, from given situations, gains which can improve their life-styles and life-chances. These are pragmatic proletarians, as their shared conditions force them to be, and they appear to accord an essential facticity to the wider order. Yet the course of political conflicts is substantially influenced by their collective weight, and their achievements are all the more noteworthy considering the short period of time in which the Ikeja labour force has been in existence. At the very least, the factory workers have the organizational capacity and the resolve to make a substantial contribution to proletarian protest movements which firmly oppose government policies and decisions and, in the course of doing so, to question the wider inequalities of Nigerian society.

The readiness of the workers to oppose the government from below cannot, however, be interpreted merely as a product of the overt relationship between themselves and those in power. Essentially, the workers' political leanings arise from their class situation at Ikeja, and the manner in which aspects of this situation ensure that it is difficult for them to make ends meet and, even more problematic, to realize their ambitions for the future. Likewise, their incipient radicalism arises from the workers' awareness of the limitations of their house unions, weaknesses to which they are well-attuned even though they are also proud of the achievements of these organizations in recent years. It is for these reasons that I have presented an assessment of the workers' political significance as a conclusion to a more extended analysis of their basic social organization, and their efforts to get by and get on in the contrasting social arenas of the Town and the Estate.

It seems appropriate to return finally to the workers in the context of the Town, and to extend on a theme raised in the opening to this chapter. This is that the sense of hostility to the wider social and political structure is by no means restricted to factory employees. The same degree of antipathy is just as vehemently articulated by the numerically preponderant self-employed townspeople, the small-scale traders, motor mechanics, electricians and others, who have the same meagre life-styles as the average wage-earner, but who do not have the same organizational ability to protest because of their very different class situation.[24]

It will be evident from a number of issues raised in this study that in several respects the workers are distinct from the majority of the self-employed poor. Their interpersonal relationships are mainly with other workers, their means of earning a livelihood contrasts with those of the self-employed, and they adhere to a proletarian sub-culture which is not appreciated by older entrepreneurs in particular. Yet this distinctiveness is only a matter of degree. Many workers have friendships with young tailors, bicycle repairers and craft apprentices, for example, and in their tenement buildings they are co-resident with self-employed men and women. Most telling of all is that those in both occupational categories have, in the main, life-styles and life-chances which are qualitatively different from those of the political class and the national bourgeoisie in the Lagos metropolitan area. Accordingly, in the course of everyday life, a sense of unity is continually articulated by wage-earners and the self-employed, a feeling of shared identity in which 'us', the urban poor at large, are judged diametrically opposed to 'them', the rich who rule in an irresponsible and voraciously self-interested fashion.

At times of industrial dispute, this empathy is frequently expressed in material aid. Workers on strike are often given food and money by self-employed friends while other acquaintances advance them cash loans to pay their rents. This occurred in early 1971, although only on occasion since most workers were involved in relatively short-lived disputes. Nevertheless, throughout the conflicts the workers resident in the Town received continuous moral support for their opposition to the government from the non-wage-earners with whom they came into contact. This pervasive empathy was often commented upon by members of both occupational categories. In the words of a young Agege electrician:

> People like myself [i.e. the self-employed] and the factory workers, we make our living in different ways. But we are also as one because we are all exploited by the Big Guns. That is why I am supporting the workers in their strike, because they have been cheated, just as we are all cheated by those in power.

Similarly, in the words of a worker on strike,

Everyone in Agege is with us in our struggle against the government. We are not just fighting for our Adebo [awards]. It is because of the way the Big Guns treat all the poor people in Nigeria that we are fighting. We are fighting for our rights and we will fight until we can fight no longer.

It is possible to object that such expressions of support cost little. It may also be argued that such encouragement is mere rhetoric. But rhetoric is a central element in political change and political conflict, and not only in Nigeria, and these expressions of support were much appreciated by the workers in the course of their struggle. They buttressed the workers' conviction that to stand firm against employers and the government was not only in their economic interests but also morally justifiable. Furthermore, the self-employed shared the workers' satisfaction in having successfully opposed the government. It was felt that those in power had acted improperly and that it was only just that the government had been forced to capitulate in the face of ordinary wage-earners' concerted opposition in Lagos and elsewhere.

So the final element of the workers' political status to which we would draw attention is that, in the course of their rebellion, they articulated a sense of generalized grievance and opposition to the structure of Nigerian society, sentiments shared by wage-earners and self-employed alike. They were raising the right of the majority of poor Nigerians to be recognized as full citizens by those who rule them. To many, the nature of Nigerian politics has been such as to suggest that the dominant class is not prepared to accord this recognition to the urban or rural poor. For this reason alone, any movement from below is to be honoured, including collective protest by factory workers. It remains to be seen whether the workers will continue to realize their massive political potential and to express the antipathy which extends well beyond their own ranks.

Notes

Preface

1 One change has been the introduction of the Naira, ₦, in place of the Nigerian pound, £N. As all figures refer to the prices at the time my fieldwork was conducted, 1970 to 1971, so the currency is given in its form at that time. In 1971 the official exchange rate of the Nigerian pound was £N1 = £1.17 = $2.80. They were exchanged for Naira at £N1 = ₦2.
2 *Report of the Tribunal of Inquiry into the Activities of Trade Unions*, (Chairman: Justice Adebiyi), Federal Ministry of Information, Lagos, 1977.
3 G. Williams, 'Nigeria: a political economy' in G. Williams (ed.), *Nigeria: Economy and Society*, Rex Collings, 1977.

Chapter 1

1 A.L. Epstein, *Politics in an Urban African Community*, Manchester University Press, 1958.
2 J.C. Mitchell, *The Kalela Dance*, Manchester University Press for the Rhodes-Livingstone Institute, Northern Rhodesia, 1956.
3 P. Mayer, *Townsmen or Tribesmen*, Oxford University Press, 1961.
4 In particular, see J.C. Mitchell, 'Theoretical Orientations in urban African studies', in *The Social Anthropology of Complex Societies*, A.S.A. Monograph No. 4 Tavistock, 1966: A.L. Epstein, 'Urbanization in Africa' *Current Anthropology*, 8, 4, 1967, 275—94; M. Gluckman, 'Anthropological problems arising from the industrial revolution in Africa', in A. Southall, (ed.), *Social Change in Modern Africa*. Oxford University Press, 1961.
5 R.D. Grillo, *African Railwaymen: Solidarity and Opposition in an East African Labour Force*. Cambridge University Press 1974; *Race Class and*

Militancy: An African Trade Union, 1939—1975. Chandler, New York, 1975.
6   D. Parkin, *Neighbours and Nationals in an African City Ward*, Routledge and Kegan Paul, 1969.
7   B. Kapferer, *Strategy and Transaction in an African Factory: African workers and Indian management in a Zambian town*, Manchester University Press, 1972.
8   P. Harries-Jones, *Freedom and Labour, Mobilization and Political Control on the Zambian Copperbelt*, Blackwell, 1976.
9   M. Banton, *West African City*, Oxford University Press for the International Africa Institute, 1957.
10 M. Peil, *The Ghanaian Factory Worker*, Cambridge University Press, 1972.
11 P.C. Lloyd, *Power and Independence: Urban Africans' Perceptions of Social Inequality*, Routledge and Kegan Paul, 1974.
12 G. Williams, 'The social stratification of a neo-colonial economy', in C.H. Allen and R.W. Johnson, (eds.), *African Perspectives: Essays in the History, Politics and Economics of Africa in honour of Thomas Hodgkin*. Cambridge University Press, 1970; 'Political consciousness amongst the Ibadan poor', in E. de Kadt and G. Williams, (eds.), *Sociology and Development*. Tavistock, 1974; 'Nigeria: a political economy' in G. Williams, (ed.) Nigeria: *Economy and Society*; 'Class relations in a neo-colony: the case of Nigeria', in P.C.W. Gutkind and P. Waterman (eds.), *African social studies: a Radical Reader*, Heinemann, 1977.
13 P.C.W. Gutkind, 'The energy of despair: social organization of the unemployed in two African cities, Lagos and Nairobi', *Civilisations*, 17, 3 & 4, 1967, 186—215, 380—405; 'From the energy of despair to the anger of despair', *Canadian Journal of African Studies*, 7, 2, 1973, 179—98; 'The view from below: political consciousness of the urban poor in Ibadan', *Cahiers d'Etudes Africaines*, 57, 1975, 5—36.
14 J.D.Y. Peel, 'Inequality and action: the forms of Ijesha social conflict', Conference on inequality in Africa. Social Science Research Council, New York, 1976.
15 R. Cohen, *Labour and Politics in Nigeria*, Heinemann, 1974.
16 *First Report of the Wages and Salaries Review Commission*. (Chairman: S.O. Adebo), Federal Ministry of Information, Lagos, 1970.
17 The standard work on the economic, social and political organization of the Yoruba kingdoms remains P.C. Lloyd, *Yoruba Land Law*, Oxford University Press for the Nigerian Institute of Social and Economic Research, 1962.

Notes

18 Most of these are from the Mid-West and Eastern States. For the sake of brevity and coherence, I do not make reference to these non-Yoruba migrants. They comprise a very small proportion of the total Ikeja labour force and are not prominent in either shopfloor or trade union affairs.
19 I hope to publish a detailed account of this survey material in the relatively near future. A preliminary description of the socio-economic characteristics of the workers and others in the Town is to be found in A.J. Peace, 'Social Change at Agege: Tribe, Status and Class in a Nigerian Township', D.Phil, thesis, University of Sussex, 1973, chapter 3. These figures, of course, refer to 1971. Since then, wages have increased, the cost of living more so.
20 Here, as subsequently, the emphasis on choice and decision-making among the migrants contrasts strongly with the position adopted by S. Amin, ('Introduction' to S. Amin, (ed.), *Modern Migrations in Western Africa*, Oxford University Press for the International Africa Institute, 1974), who argues that West African migrants have no choice but to migrate from rural to urban areas. Amin's position, however, is not clearly formulated and he appears to confuse the rate of migration with its incidence.
21 For Southern Africa, see A.L. Epstein, *Politics in an Urban African Community*; J.C. Mitchell, 'Theoretical orientations in urban African studies'; H. Heisler, 'A class of target proletarians', *Journal of African and Asian Studies*, 5, 3, 1970, 161–75; *Urbanization and the Government of Migration: the Interrelation of Urban and Rural Life in Zambia*, Cambridge University Press, 1974. For an East African example, see W. Elkan, *Migrants and Proletarians: Urban Labour in the Economic Development of Uganda*, Oxford University Press, 1960.
22 Here, as elsewhere, I have relied on the two complementary studies by R.D. Grillo, *African Railwaymen*, and *Race, Class and Militancy*, which together seem to me to provide the most comprehensive account of an African wage-earning population to have appeared in recent years.
23 R. Sandbrook and R. Cohen, (eds.), *The Development of an African Working Class: Studies in Class Formation and Action*, Longmans, 1975, 132.

Chapter 2

1   For example, M. Banton, *West African City*; M. Fraenkel, *Tribe and Class in Monrovia*, Oxford University Press for the International Africa Institute, 1964.

2   D. Parkin, *Neighbours and Nationals in an African City Ward*, Routledge and Kegan Paul, 1969.
3   A. Cohen, *Custom and Politics in Urban Africa: a study of Hausa migrants in Yoruba towns*, Routledge and Kegan Paul, 1969.
4   P.C. Lloyd, 'Craft organization in Yoruba towns', *Africa*, 33, 1, 1953, 30–44; E. Krapf-Askari, *Yoruba Towns and Cities*, Clarendon Press, 1969.
5   The notion of encapsulation was most effectively employed in his classic study of Red Xhosa in East London by P. Mayer, *Townsmen or Tribesmen*, Oxford University Press, 1961. It would be inapposite to Agege where immigrants feel that an important benefit of Town residence is the experience gained from personal contact with migrants from Yoruba kingdoms other than their own.
6   It will be evident that I employ the term 'social network' in a relatively elementary descriptive sense. For considerably more complex and sophisticated usages, see the various contributions to J.C. Mitchell, (ed.), *Social Networks in Urban Situations*, Manchester University Press, 1969.
7   By way of illustration of this relative homogeneity, the following table gives a breakdown of six social networks in my own locality. The data on all six groups were recorded during the same month, and during this time networks 1, 3 and 6 each contained one unemployed member:

Number of network:	Number in network:	Ethnic identity:	Age range of members (yrs)	Length of time in Agege (mnths)	Income range £N (1971)
1	4	Egba	18–22	12–36	£10–£12.15s.
2	3	Ekiti	19–21	6–18	£10–£11.10s.
3	5	Egba/Lagos	19–23	3–30	£10–£13
4	2	Oyo	20–22	24–30	£12–£12.10s.
5	4	Ijebu	18–21	8–24	£10–£13. 5s.
6	4	Egbado	17–20	18–36	£10–£13.15s.

8   I should at least acknowledge not having enquired closely enough as to why migrants invite guests to join them at all, for in certain respects they appear to be saddling themselves with an unnecessary burden. The feature which is especially crucial is that existing Agege residents and new arrivals are intimate

friends and as such it behoves the former to assist the latter in escaping from the limitations of their place of origin. Furthermore, migrants gain some degree of prestige as well as personal satisfaction from helping friends in this fashion. A point which is suggested, though not clearly established by survey material, is that there is a gradual transition underway to assisting junior siblings to enter Agege rather than close friends. As yet only a small minority of migrants have siblings in Town; this is to be expected in that, as noted elsewhere, most are first sons with junior siblings still at school. As the latter end their secondary education, one might anticipate that migrants will increasingly assist siblings rather than friends to enter the modern urban milieu. For the present, when asked why they invite others to join them in Town, the usual response is on the lines, 'He is my close friend and as such I must help him all I can'.

Chapter 3

1   P.C. Lloyd, *Power and Independence*, ch. 2 and 3.
2   On 'imitable models' see S.F. Nadel. 'The idea of a social elite', *International Social Science Bulletin*, 8, 1956, 413–24.
3   I refer in the text only to the majority of Yoruba entrepreneurs. Agege has a substantial Hausa population and many of these are self-employed businessmen, some of them quite as prosperous and powerful as their Yoruba counterparts. In the present study, I have omitted reference to this population since they comprise a very distinctive ethnic group, organized on much the same lines as the Hausa community of Ibadan described in A. Cohen, *Custom and Politics*. Moreover, Hausa migrants do not seek employment in the Ikeja factories. Other considerations apart, their lack of Western education automatically excludes them from such employment.
4   The term 'spiralist' has been accorded a variety of usages by anthropologists and sociologists. In this context, I simply refer to individuals who are experiencing a notable degree of socio-economic mobility and are thus regarded by those around them.
5   I have tried to explore at least some of the complexities of socio-economic differentiation in Agege in A.J. Peace, 'Prestige, power and legitimacy'.
6   The contrasts seem especially striking when set against accounts of East and Southern African migrants. Doubtless, there are several reasons why this should be so. One may be that other African labour forces generally contain

a higher proportion of middle aged wage-earners who value highly ties with their villages of origin for reasons of prestige and because their retirement to them is relatively imminent. In East and Southern Africa, close attention to the affairs of village-based kinsmen appears inextricably bound up with the retention of rights in land, particularly in areas of land shortage. By contrast, land for cultivation is relatively freely available in Yorubaland and full property-rights are retained notwithstanding a migrant's length of absence. Most obviously, Agege wage-earners simply do not have the income resources to participate in home town and village affairs to the same degree as their East and Southern African counterparts.

7   A further cost may arise in the payment of bride price which can be as much as £N20 to £N25. Generally, however, it appears that this is borne by a migrant's parents or is waived altogether.

8   See A.J. Peace, 'Social Change at Agege', ch. 3.

Chapter 4

1   On the limited aspirations of the British working class, the major anthropological study of the influence of the work situation and wider community relationships is still N. Dennis, F. Henriques and C. Slaughter, *Coal is our Life*, second edn., Tavistock, 1969 (first edn., 1956), while R. Hoggart, *The Uses of Literacy*, Penguin, 1966, remains invaluable. See also M. Mann, (ed.), *Working Class Images*, Routledge and Kegan Paul, 1976. There is however some indication that within the more geographically mobile sections of the working class in advanced industrial societies, aspirations for the future include that of becoming self-employed. E. Chinoy, *The Automobile Workers and the American Dream*, Doubleday, 1966; D. Lockwood, J. Goldthorpe, F. Bechoffer and J. Platt, *The Affluent Worker: Industrial Attitudes and Behaviour*, Cambridge University Press, 1968, and A. Touraine and O. Ragazzi, *Ouvrier d'Origine Agricole*, Laboratoire de Sociologie Industrielle et l'Ecole Pratique des Hautes Etudes, Paris, 1961, all document such aspirations amongst the members of the American, British and French working class respectively.

2   I have borrowed this presentational technique from R.D. Grillo, *African Railwaymen*, but also amended it, in that his account of subjective occupational rank appears to draw primarily on the emphases of those in the higher ranks of the East African Railways and Harbours.

Notes 183

3   The same point has been made by reference to the shared stereotypes of ethnic categories by J.C. Mitchell, *The Kalela Dance*, and 'Theoretical orientations in urban African Studies', and others. It is evident that the course and content of categorical relationships among workers is greatly complicated by the influence of both perceived occupational rank and ethnic identity in ephemeral encounters. I have found it necessary to omit these complications, since to do otherwise would greatly lengthen discussion of a subsidiary theme in this chapter.

4   In the following section, the distinctions between work, status and market situation follow those developed by D. Lockwood, *The Blackcoated Worker: a Study in Class Consciousness*, Allen and Unwin, 1958.

5   Under certain circumstances, skilled workers do not even find it necessary to approach or otherwise pressure their employers for wage increases, following general increments on the shopfloor. Following the resolution of the Adebo affair described in Chapter 6, several European firms immediately awarded their skilled workers increases of a similar order to those fought for by the shopfloor men. Others did so after only the slightest representation from foremen and chargehands, even though some of these had incomes above the upper limit recommended by the Adebo Commission. Such is the worth of skilled workers to their employers.

6   Since skilled workers' bargaining techniques are employed in 'closed settings', that is, in private conversations between a worker and his immediate management superior, this account draws heavily on conversations with such workers and with expatriate managers. For this reason, I cannot give an appropriate illustration. However, apropos the fact that skilled workers may prefer the stability and routinization of their current employment to fully maximising on their wider market situation, a brief example is possible. It concerns a senior chargehand of some seven years employment in the same factory, on an income of £N58 per month, and owning a growing business in cement and roofing materials managed on a day to day basis by his wife. As much out of interest as serious intent, he applied for the position of foreman in a newly opened factory on the Ilupeju Industrial Estate south of Ikeja. He was immediately offered the post with a basic monthly income of £N72 and the assurance of an even higher regular wage since the management required all skilled men to work overtime, including weekends. It was precisely the latter consideration which led the chargehand to set aside any further thought of moving to another factory; it was at the weekends that he was able fully to assume the mantle of the urban business man.

7   In particular see R. Sandbrook, *Proletarians and African Capitalism: the Kenya case 1962–1970*, Cambridge University Press, 1975, an important account of the labour movement in Kenya, more concerned as it is with trade union organization and trade unions than with proletarians as such. See also the contributions to R. Sandbrook and R. Cohen, (eds.), *The Development of an African Working Class*. Several essays in this volume specifically address themselves to the question of whether African wage-earners comprise a distinctive proletarian class. Yet all are perhaps overly concerned with answering the question with reference to union organization and industrial and political action, including my own, 'The Lagos proletariat: labour aristocrats or populist militants?'. On the other hand, the authors all rightly eschew the tangential, if not irrelevant, line of argument that African workers are not properly termed proletarians because they retain interests in village land and rural affairs.
8   For example, N. Dennis *et al*, *Coal is our Life*; H. Beynon, *Working for Ford*, Penguin, 1973.
9   For example, A.L. Epstein, *Politics in an Urban African Community*; R. Grillo, *Race, Class and Militancy*; R.H. Bates, *Unions, Parties and Political Development: A Study of Mineworkers in Zambia*, Yale University Press, 1971; and R. Sandbrook, *Proletarians and African Capitalism*.

Chapter 5

1   Alternatively one might argue that the lack of cooperation and combination between Ikeja employers has not provided an appropriate stimulus for a drawing together of the various strands of the labour movement. It is this feature of the Ikeja Estate which contrasts most strongly with the 'unitary structures' so common in other industrial centres in sub-Saharan Africa for there is no doubt that, notwithstanding their multi-national character, Ikeja firms are engaged in strong competition between themselves and/or others elsewhere in the country. A further source of division within the ranks of the Ikeja employers is of a specifically political nature. European employers in general are most hostile to non-European ones since they feel that, because the latter make no effort to disguise the extreme exploitation to which they subject their employees, so they bring into disrepute expatriate employers as a whole and allow the government every possible justification for far more direct involvement in the manufacturing sector. Since 1971 these fears have been realized to a considerable extent.

Notes

2   *Report of the Commission on the Review of Wages, Salaries and Conditions of Service of the Junior Employees of the Governments of the Federation and in Private Establishment, 1963–1964*: (Chairman: Mr. Justice Adeyinka Morgan), Federal Ministry of Information, Lagos, 1964.

3   There are several accounts of the 1964 General Strike though one suspects that much more material could be unearthed on this critically important event. For the present there are useful accounts by E.R. Braundi and A. Letteri, 'The general strike in Nigeria', *International Socialist Journal*, 1, 1964, 598–609; R. Melson, 'Nigerian politics and the general strike of 1964', in R.I. Rotberg and A.A. Mazrui, (eds.), *Protest and Power in Black Africa*, Oxford University Press, New York, 1970; and R. Cohen, *Labour and Politics in Nigeria*. W. Ananaba, *The Trade Union Movement in Nigeria*, Hurst, 1969, offers an intriguing if idiosyncratic account from inside the national leadership.

4   It should be added that while all elected officials are unpaid, some house unions pay a small monthly income to professional trade unionists in order to relieve their presidents of time-consuming administrative tasks. These 'general secretaries' perform in a similar capacity for several house unions at a time and thus put together a reasonable income. For a detailed account of the characteristics and activities of these figures, see R. Cohen, *Labour and Politics in Nigeria*. Cohen is, for the most part, concerned with unionism in the public sector where the influence and authority of general secretaries is evidently far greater than in the private sector.

5   House union presidents are generally at one with ordinary workers in sharing the ambition of self-employment. A consideration of importance is that, since they are also what I have termed established workers, they are concerned to save from somewhat higher incomes but find this especially difficult. Many costs can be incurred through attendance at the numerous social activities to which they are invited by their followers. These costs, plus the pressures of leadership, led some presidents to tell me that they intended to remain active unionists for only a few years before resigning and committing themselves to saving with a view to self-employment. I do not know whether such voluntary retirements from office have transpired since 1971.

6   These attendance figures are on a par with rates for trade union meetings in modern industrial societies. They are a matter of concern to union leaders since, in their view, meetings serve an invaluable safety-valve function. For this reason, presidents often convene emergency meetings at their factory gates to coincide with the change in shifts and thus to capture some two-

thirds of their work forces. In the days preceding the 1971 disputes described in Chapter 6, such meetings became relatively commonplace on the Estate and were crucially important in keeping leaders in touch with majority opinion.

7 In line with the pattern in most African trade union movements, Ikeja unionism is generally free of ethnic or tribal influences. During the period of my fieldwork, the tribal factor only arose when members explained their presidents' different styles of leadership in terms of ethnic stereotypes. Thus one president was considered especially aggressive 'because that is the way with Ijebu men' whilst another was felt to be particularly shrewd in his dealings with management since 'like all Ekiti he is devious and likes to play politics'.

8 Government minimum wage and Lagos consumer price index for lower income workers, 1960–1976. Base year 1960:

Year	Daily wage (£N, £N1 = ₦2)	Money wage (a) index	Price index food	Price index all items (b)	'Real wage' (a) ÷ (b)
1960	5s.10d.	100	100	100	100
1961	5s.10d.	100	108	105	75
1962	5s.10d.	100	114	110	91
1963	5s.10d.	100	106	109	92
1964	5s.10d.–7s.8d.	100–132	110	112	89–118
1965	7s.8d.	132	114	117	113
1966	7s.8d.	132	131	127	104
1967	7s.8d.	132	119	122	108
1968	7s.8d.	132	117	123	107
1969	7s.8d.	132	138	136	97
1970	7s.8d.–9s.5d.	132–162	166	154	86–105
1971	9s.5d.–10s.	162–172	204	175	93–98
1972	10s. = ₦1	172	209	181	95
1973	₦1	172	212	186	92
1974	₦1–₦2	172–344	248	218	79–158
1975	₦2	344	362	287	120
1976	₦2 (= £N1)	344	448	343	100

Sources: Figures on prices derived from publications of the Central Bank of Nigeria, the Federal Office of Statistics and the United Nations Statistical Yearbooks. Although they purport to derive from the same source, namely the Consumer price Surveys of the Federal Office of Statistics, they are not always consistent with each other, especially for food prices. The 'real wage' index is constructed as though prices were con-

Notes

stant within each year, which is, of course, not the case. Price and 'real wage' indicators should be treated as rough indicators. I am grateful to Peter Waterman for making available an index constructed for an unpublished paper on the Nigerian Ports Authority. For a table giving figures for 1939–1970, see R. Cohen, *Labour and Politics in Nigeria*, table 6.1, 192.

9   Doubtless certain employers found the argument of low profitability a useful one with which simply to stave off union leaders' demands. At the same time it is indisputable that for others, including some of the largest companies, changes in government policy were causing real difficulties. This was indicated by the fact that in 1970 and 1971 several major firms had, at least temporarily, shelved ambitious development programmes drawn up during the later stages of the civil war. Furthermore, not long after I completed my research, at least two leading European firms undertook substantial restructuring of their factories to meet the worst effects of changes in import policy. On the fall in manufacturing output and especially cotton textiles in 1971 and 1972, see International Monetary Fund, *Survey of African Economics*, vol. 6. Washington D.C., 1975, p. 299.

10 The distinctly authoritarian nature of leadership is a recurrent feature in the literature on African trade unionism. See, in particular, the concluding chapter to R.D. Grillo, *Race, Class and Militancy*. In some instances, the extent of authoritarianism appears so great that one wonders why ordinary members bother to attend meetings and otherwise tolerate quite dictatorial control, as in the Nigerian Mine Workers Union described by D.R. Smock, *Conflict and Control in an African Trade Union*, Hoover Institution Press, Stanford, 1969.

Chapter 6

1   It might be added here that in the course of the book we have been describing a different type of migrant wage-earner to those already prominent in the anthropological literature. Notably, the Ikeja workers contrast with the 'target workers' of Southern and East Africa in the 1950s as described by A.L. Epstein, J.C. Mitchell, and W. Elkan. The Ikeja workers certainly share a common 'target', but it is that of urban self-employment and not to return to their places of origin with cash in hand. However, the sociology and historiography of African mine labour in particular has been rewritten in recent years by several Marxist writers, starting with Giovanni Arrighi's seminal

essay, 'Labour Supplies in Historical Perspective', now reprinted in G. Arrighi and J. Saul, *The Political Economy of Africa*, Monthly Review Press, 1973. See also the essays contained in R. Palmer and N. Parsons (eds.), *The Roots of Rural Poverty*, Heinemann, 1977 and, most important, Charles van Onselen, *Chibaro: African Mineworkers in Southern Rhodesia, 1900–1933*, Pluto Press, 1976. This study in particular disputes the suggestion that early migrants moved with some degree of freedom and choice between rural and urban areas — as is implied by the very concept of 'target employment'.

The Ikeja workers' circumstances also stand in marked contrast to those of the 'labour aristocrat' railwaymen of Kampala described by R.D. Grillo in *African Railwaymen* and *Race, Class and Militancy*. The comparisons with these very prosperous and secure government employees are obvious enough, though one doubts that they enjoy today the same circumstances as they did in the early 1960s.

Some parallels might be drawn between Ikeja workers and the wage-earners studied by Margaret Peil (1972) in Ghana and Bruce Kapferer (1972) in Zambia, for some of these aspire to owning their own business enterprises. In neither case however do they seem to share, to the same degree, the uniform ambition found amongst Ikeja workers. From Margaret Peil's book, *Ghanaian Factory Worker*, it appears that only some of her subjects share the Ikeja workers' ambition of self-employment. I have not been able to consult a recent publication by Richard Jeffries, *Class, Power and Ideology in Ghana*, Cambridge University Press, 1977.

2 Some aspects of the social organization of the self-employed are described in my paper, 'Prestige, Power and Legitimacy in a Modern Nigerian Town', presented to the Burg Wartenstein Symposium, No. 73. A revised version will shortly appear in the *Canadian Journal of African Studies.*

3 An invaluable description of the physical and social ecology of metropolitan Lagos is to be found in A.L. Mabogunje, *Urbanization in Nigeria*, University of London Press, 1968.

4 On the *Agbekoya* movement, see C.E.F. Beer, *The Politics of Peasant Groups in Western Nigeria*, Ibadan University Press, 1976; C.E.F. Beer and G. Williams, 'The Politics of the Ibadan Peasantry', in G. Williams (ed.), *Nigeria: Economy and Society*; and G. Williams, 'Political Consciousness among the Ibadan Poor'.

5 The factory workers of Kano are the subject of Paul Lubeck's 'Early Industrialization and Social Class Formation in Kano, Nigeria', Ph.D. thesis,

Northwestern University, 1975. See also his essay, 'Unions, Workers and Consciousness in Kano, Nigeria', in R. Sandbrook and R. Cohen (eds.), *The Development of an African Working Class.*

6   On the Ibadan self-employed, see G. Williams, 'Political Consciousness amongst the Ibadan Poor', and P.C. Lloyd, *Power and Independence.* Also P.C.W. Gutkind, 'From the Energy of Despair to the Anger of Despair: The Transition from Social Circulation to Political Consciousness among the Poor in Urban Africa', *Canadian Journal of African Studies,* 7, 2, 1975; and 'The View from Below: Political Consciousness of the Urban Poor in Ibadan', *Cahiers d'Etudes Africaines,* 15, 1, 1975. For a more wide-ranging survey account covering four urban centres, see M. Peil, *Nigerian Politics: the Peoples' View,* Longmans, 1976.

7   See for example, the essays by P.C.W. Gutkind, 'From the Energy of Despair to the Anger of Despair' and 'The View from Below', in which attempts are made to marry an apparently Marxist perspective with material drawn from formal interviews. The unsatisfactory results have been succinctly outlined by J.D.Y. Peel in his most stimulating paper, 'Inequality and Action: the Forms of Ijesha Social Conflict', (unpublished).

8   From the preface to *Politics and Change: Orissa in 1959,* Manchester University Press, 1963.

9   Godfrey Wilson's study, *An Essay on the Economics of Detribalization,* Rhodes-Livingstone Institute Paper No. 5, 1941, remains the classic statement by an Africanist of the need to locate a local-level population within the wider system of class relationships. Abner Cohen has argued that the social anthropologist 'must deliberately formulate his problems in such a way as to make reference to the state a necessary part of his analysis', in 'Political Anthropology: the Analysis of the Symbolism of Power Relationships', *Man* (N.S.) 4, 1, 1968. Joan Vincent in a useful review article 'Urbanization in Africa', *Journal of Commonwealth and Comparative Politics,* 3, 1976, has also advocated closer attention to class relationships, political conflict and political consciousness.

10 On the lines of, for example, G. Williams, 'Nigeria: a Political Economy'; and G. Williams and T. Turner, 'Nigeria', in J. Dunn (ed.), *West African States: Failure and Promise,* Cambridge University Press, 1978.

11 See R. Luckham, *The Nigerian Military,* Cambridge University Press, 1971.

12 These measures are comprehensively described in Peter Kilby, *Industrialization in an Open Economy: Nigeria, 1945–1966,* Cambridge University Press, 1969. See also J.F. Weeks, 'Employment, growth and foreign domi-

nation in underdeveloped countries', *Review of Radical Political Economics*, 4, 1, 1972, for a critical assessment of the worth of such measures.

13 The emphasis is on the apparent nature of such prospects in 1970 since, by early 1978, after some eight years of massive government spending, the picture is very different. A number of major projects set up in the post-war euphoria are now faced with financial stringency, for example the new universities. The government is attempting to raise large overseas loans, and running into serious difficulties in doing so. The country's financial reserves are being depleted while oil exports are falling and revenues are declining relative to imports.

14 See R. Cohen, *Labour and Politics in Nigeria*, Table 6.2, 194.

15 The United Committee for Central Labour Organizations, *Equitable Demand for Economic Growth and National Prosperity*, Government Printer, Ibadan 1970.

16 Adebo (Interim) Report, *First Report of the Wages and Salaries Review Commission*, Federal Ministry of Information, Lagos, 1970, 11.

17 *ibid.*

18 For developments in Kano among predominantly non-unionized labour forces, see Paul Lubeck, 'Early Industrialization and Social Class Formation among Factory Workers in Kano, Nigeria'. For a more general account, see the penultimate chapter to Robin Cohen, *Labour and Politics in Nigeria*.

19 The Indigenization Decree of 1972 was followed by another in 1976 which went considerably further in placing control of profitable manufacturing and trading activities in the hands of indigenous businessmen and others. See P. Collins, 'The State and dependent capitalist development: The Nigerian experience', *Journal of Comparative and Commonwealth Politics*.

20 E.P. Thompson, *The Making of the English Working Class*, Penguin, 1968, 9.

21 A.G. Hopkins, 'The Lagos Strike of 1897: an Exploration in Nigerian Labour History', *Past and Present*, 35, 1966.

22 A. Hughes and R. Cohen, *Towards the Emergence of a Nigerian Working Class*, Occasional Paper, Series D, no. 7, Faculty of Commerce and Social Science, University of Birmingham, 1971.

23 These historical developments are lucidly described in Robin Cohen, *Labour and Politics in Nigeria*.

24 This secondary theme I have elaborated in 'The Lagos Proletariat: Labour Aristocrats or Populist Militants?', where it was developed as part of a critique of the 'labour aristocracy thesis'. To repeat the debate here would seem unnecessary in the light of the subsequent weight of criticism of that thesis

which has appeared from several quarters. For a summary of this material, and an excellent review of the available literature on the political status of Africa's wage-earning populations, see R. Sandbrook, 'The Political Potential of African Urban Workers', *Canadian Journal of African Studies*, vol. 9, 3, 1977.

Bibliography

ADEBIYI Report, *Report of the Tribunal of Inquiry into the Activities of Trade Unions*. Federal Ministry of Information, Lagos, 1977.

ADEBO (Interim) Report, *First Report of the Wages and Salaries Review Commission*, Federal Ministry of Information, Lagos, 1970.

ADEBO (Final) Report, *Second and Final Report of the Wages and Salaries Review Commission*, Federal Ministry of Information, Lagos, 1971.

ALLEN, V.L. 'The meaning of the working class in Africa', *Journal of Modern African Studies*, 10, 2, 1972, 169–89.

AMIN, S. (ed.), *Modern Migrations in Western Africa*, Oxford University Press for the International African Institute, London, 1974.

ANANABA, W., *The Trade Union Movement in Nigeria*, Hurst, 1969.

ARONSON, D.A., 'Ijebu Yoruba urban-rural relationships and class formation', *Canadian Journal of African Studies*, 5, 1971, 263–79.

ARRIGHI, G. & SAUL, J., *Essays on the Political Economy of Africa*, Monthly Review Press, 1973.

BAILEY, F.G., *Politics and Social Change: Orissa in 1959*, Manchester University Press, 1963.

BANTON, M., *West African City*, Oxford University Press for the International Africa Institute, 1957.

BATES, R.H., *Unions, Parties and Political Development: A Study of Mineworkers in Zambia*, Yale University Press, 1971.

BEYNON, H., *Working for Ford*, Penguin, 1973.

BRAUNDI, E.R., and LETTERI, A., 'The general strike in Nigeria', *International Socialist Journal*, 1, 1964, 598–609.

CHINOY, E., *Automobile Workers and the American Dream*, Doubleday, 1955.

COHEN, A., *Custom and Politics in Urban Africa: a study of Hausa migrants in Yoruba towns*, Routledge and Kegan Paul, 1969.

COHEN, A., 'Political anthropology: the analysis of the symbolism of power relations', *Man* (N.S.), 4, 1, 1969, 216–35.
COHEN, A. (ed.), *Urban Ethnicity*, A.S.A. Monograph 12, Tavistock, 1974.
COHEN, R., & MICHAEL, D., 'The revolutionary potential of the lumpenproletariat: a sceptical view', *Bulletin of the Institute of Development Studies*, 5, 2–3, 1973, 31–42.
COHEN, R., *Labour and Politics in Nigeria*, Heinemann, 1974.
COLLINS, P., 'The state and dependent capitalist development: The Nigerian experience', *Journal of Comparative and Commonwealth Politics*, 15, 2, 1977, 127–50.
DAVIES, I., *African Trade Unions*, Penguin, 1966.
DENNIS, N., HENRIQUES, F., & SLAUGHTER, C., *Coal is our Life*, second edition, Tavistock, 1969.
ELKAN, W., *Migrants and Proletarians: Urban Labour in the Economic Development of Uganda*, Oxford University Press, 1960.
EPSTEIN, A.L., *Politics in an Urban African Community*, Manchester University Press, 1958.
EPSTEIN, A.L., 'Urbanization in Africa', *Current Anthropology*, 8, 4, 1967, 275–94.
FANON, F., *The Wretched of the Earth*, Penguin, 1967.
FRAENKEL, M., *Tribe and Class in Monrovia*, Oxford University Press for the International African Institute, 1964.
GARBETT, K., 'Circulatory labour migration in Rhodesia: towards a decision model', in D. Parkin (ed.), *Town and Country in Central and East Africa*, Oxford University Press, 1975.
GARBETT, K., 'Labour migration and development in the Lower Shire Valley, Malawi, in historical perspective', *Proceedings of the Seminar on Migration and Rural Development in Tropical Africa*, Afrika Studiecentrum Leiden, 1977.
GERTH, H.H. & MILLS, C.W. (eds.), *From Max Weber: Essays in Sociology*, Routledge and Kegan Paul, 1967.
GLUCKMAN, M., 'Anthropological problems arising from the industrial revolution in Africa', in Southall, A., (ed.), *Social Change in Modern Africa*, Oxford University Press, 1961.
GRILLO, R.D., *African Railwaymen: Solidarity and Opposition in an East African Labour Force*, Cambridge University Press, 1974.
GRILLO, R.D., *Race, Class and Militancy: An African Trade Union, 1939–1965*, Chandler, New York, 1975.

GUTKIND, P.C.W., 'The energy of despair: social organization of the unemployed in two African cities, Lagos and Nairobi', *Civilisations*, 17, 3 & 4, 1967, 186–215, 380–405.

GUTKIND, P.C.W., 'From the energy of despair to the anger of despair', *Canadian Journal of African Studies*, 7, 2, 1973, 179–98.

GUTKIND, P.C.W., 'The view from below: political consciousness of the urban poor in Ibadan', *Cahiers d'Etudes Africaines*, 57, 1975, 5–36.

GUTKIND, P.C.W., *The Emergent African Proletariat*, Occasional Paper No. 8., Center for Developing Area Studies, McGill University, 1974.

HARRIES-JONES, P.J.C., *Freedom and Labour, Mobilization and political control on the Zambian copperbelt*, Blackwell, 1975.

HEISLER, H., 'A class of target proletarians', *Journal of African and Asian Studies*, 5, 3, 1970, 161–75.

HEISLER, H., *Urbanization and the Government of Migration: the Interrelation of Urban and Rural Life in Zambia*, Cambridge University Press, 1974.

HINCHLIFFE, K., 'Labour aristocracy – A Northern Nigerian case study', *Journal of Modern African Studies*, 12, 1, 1974, 57–67.

HOBSBAWM, E.J., 'Class consciousness in History', in Meszaros, I., (ed.), *Aspects of History and Class Consciousness*, Routledge and Kegan Paul, 1971.

HOGGART, R., *The Uses of Literacy*, Penguin, 1966.

HOPKINS, A.G., 'The Lagos strike of 1897: an exploration in Nigerian labour history', *Past and Present*, 35, 1966, 135–55.

HUGHES, A. & COHEN, R., *Towards the Emergence of a Nigerian Working Class*, Occasional Paper, Series D. No. 7, Faculty of Commerce and Social Science, University of Birmingham, 1971.

INTERNATIONAL MONETARY FUND, *Survey of African Economies*, vol. 6. Washington, D.C. 1975.

JEFFRIES, R., 'Populist tendencies in the Ghanaian trade union movement', in R. Sandbrook and R. Cohen, (eds.), *The Development of an African Working Class*, Longmans, 1975.

KAPFERER, B., *Strategy and Transaction in an African Factory: African workers and Indian management in a Zambian town*, Manchester University Press, 1972.

KILBY, P., *Industrialization in an Open Economy: Nigeria, 1945–1966*, Cambridge University Press, 1969.

KRAPF-ASKARI, E., *Yoruba Towns and Cities*, Clarendon Press, 1969.

LITTLE, K., *West African Urbanization*, Cambridge University Press, 1969.

LITTLE, K., *Urbanization as a Social Problem: an Essay on Movement and Change in Contemporary Africa*, Routledge and Kegan Paul, 1974.

LOCKWOOD, D., *The Blackcoated Worker: a study in class consciousness*, Allen and Unwin, 1958.

LOCKWOOD, D., GOLDTHORPE, J., BECHOFFER, F., & PLATT, J., *The Affluent Worker: Industrial Attitudes and Behaviour*, Cambridge University Press, 1968.

LLOYD, P.C., 'Craft organization in Yoruba towns', *Africa*, 33, 1, 1953, 30–44.

LLOYD, P.C., *Yoruba Land Law*, Oxford University Press for the Nigerian Institute of Social and Economic Research, 1962.

LLOYD, P.C., 'Introduction' and 'Class consciousness among the Yoruba', in Lloyd, P.C. (ed.), *The New Elites of Tropical Africa*, Oxford University Press for the International African Institute, 1966.

LLOYD, P.C., *Africa in Social Change*, Penguin, 1967.

LLOYD, P.C., *Power and Independence: Urban Africans' Perceptions of Social Inequality*, Routledge and Kegan Paul, 1974.

LUBECK, P., 'Unions, workers and consciousness in Kano, Nigeria: a view from below', in R. Sandbrook and R. Cohen, (eds.), *The Development of an African Working Class*, Longmans, 1975.

LUBECK, P., 'Early industrialization and social class formation among factory workers in Kano', Ph.D. thesis, Northwestern University, 1975.

LUCKHAM, R., *The Nigerian Military*, Cambridge University Press, 1971.

MABOGUNJE, A.L., *Urbanization in Nigeria*, University of London Press, 1968.

MANN, M., (ed.), *Working Class Images*, Routledge and Kegan Paul, 1976.

MAYER, P., *Townsmen or Tribesmen*, Oxford University Press, 1961.

MELSON, R., 'Nigerian politics and the general strike of 1964', in Rotberg, R.J. & Mazrui, A.A., (eds.), *Protest and Power in Black Africa*, Oxford University Press, New York, 1970.

MITCHELL, J.C., 'The causes of labour migration', *Bulletin of the International African Labour Institute*, 6, 1952, 12–47.

MITCHELL, J.C., *The Kalela Dance*, Manchester University Press for the Rhodes-Livingstone Institute, Northern Rhodesia, 1956.

MITCHELL, J.C., 'Theoretical orientations in urban African studies', in Banton, M., (ed.), *The Social Anthropology of Complex Societies*, A.S.A. Monograph No. 4, Tavistock, 1966.

MITCHELL, J.C., *Social Networks in Urban Situations*, Manchester University Press, 1969.

MORGAN Report, *Report of the Commission on the Review of Wages, Salaries and Conditions of Service of the Junior Employees of the Governments of the Federation and In Private Establishments, 1963–1964*, Federal Ministry of Information, Lagos, 1964.
NADEL, S.F., 'The idea of a social elite', *International Social Science Bulletin*, 8, 1956, 413–424.
PALMER, R. and PARSONS, N., *The Roots of Rural Poverty*, Heinemann, 1977.
PARKIN, D., *Neighbours and Nationals in an African City Ward*, Routledge and Kegan Paul, 1969.
PARKIN, D., (ed.), *Town and Country in Central and Eastern Africa*, Oxford University Press for the International African Institute, 1975.
PEACE, A.J., 'Social Change at Agege: Tribe, Status and Class in a Nigerian Township', D.Phil. thesis, University of Sussex, 1973.
PEACE, A.J., 'The Lagos proletariat: labour aristocrats or populist militants?' in R. Sandbrook and R. Cohen, (eds.), *The Development of an African Working Class*, Longmans, 1975.
PEACE, A.J., 'Prestige, power and legitimacy in a modern Nigerian town', Symposium No. 73, *Shanty Towns in Developing Nations*, Wenner-Gren Foundation for Anthropological Research, New York, 1977, to be published in a revised version in *Canadian Journal of African Studies*, forthcoming.
PEEL, J.D.Y., *Aladura: a Religious Movement among the Yoruba*, Oxford University Press for the International African Institute, 1968.
PEEL, J.D.Y., 'Inequality and Action: the forms of Ijesha Conflict', Conference on inequality in Africa, Social Science Research Council, New York, 1976.
PEIL, M., *The Ghanaian Factory Worker*, Cambridge University Press, 1972.
PEIL, M., *Nigerian Politics: the Peoples' View*, Longmans, 1976.
SANDBROOK, R., *Proletarians and African Capitalism: the Kenya Case, 1962–1970*, Cambridge University Press, 1975.
SANDBROOK, R., 'The political potential of African urban workers', *Canadian Journal of African Studies*, 9, 3, 1977.
SMOCK, D.R., *Conflict and Control in an African Trade Union*, Hoover Institution Press, Stanford, 1969.
THOMPSON, E.P., *The Making of the English Working Class*, Penguin, 1968.
TOURAINE, A. & RAGAZZI, O., *Ouvriers d'Origine Agricole*, Laboratoire de Sociologie Industrielle de l'Ecole Pratique des Hautes Etudes, Paris, 1961.
TOYO, E., *The Working Class and the Nigerian Crisis*, Sketch Publishing Company, Ibadan, n.d.

UNITED COMMITTEE FOR CENTRAL LABOUR ORGANIZATIONS (U.C.C.L.O.), *Equitable Demand for Economic Growth and National Prosperity*, Government Printer, Ibadan, 1970.
VAN ONSELEN, C., *Chibaro: African Mine Labour in Southern Rhodesia, 1900–1933*, Pluto Press, 1976.
VINCENT, J., 'Urbanization in Africa', *Journal of Commonwealth and Comparative Politics*, 14, 3, 1976, 287–98.
WATERMAN, P., *Industrial Relations and the Control of Labour Protest in Nigeria*, Institute of Social Studies, The Hague, 1976.
WEEKS, J.F., 'Employment, growth and foreign domination in underdeveloped countries', *Review of Radical Political Economics*, 4, 1, 1972, 59–70.
WOLPE, H., *Urban Politics in Nigeria: a Study of Port Harcourt*, University of California Press, 1978.
WOODIS, J., *Theories of Revolution*, Lawrence and Wishart, 1970.
WILLIAMS, G., 'The social stratification of a neo-colonial economy: Western Nigeria', in Allen, C.H., and Johnson, R.W. (eds.), *African Perspectives: Essays in the History, Politics and Economics of Africa in honour of Thomas Hodgkin*, Cambridge University Press, 1970.
WILLIAMS, G., 'Political consciousness among the Ibadan poor', in de Ka t, E., and Williams, G., (eds.), *Sociology and Development*, Tavistock, 1974.
WILLIAMS, G., 'Nigeria: a political economy' in Williams, G. (ed.), *Nigeria: Economy and Society*, Rex Collings, 1976.
WILLIAMS, G., 'Class relations in a neo-colony: the case of Nigeria', in Gutkind, P.C.W. and Waterman, P. (eds.), *African Social Studies: a Radical Reader*, Heinemann, 1977.
WILLIAMS, G. and TURNER, T., 'Nigeria' in Dunn, J. (ed.), *West African states: failure and promise*, Cambridge University Press, 1978.
WILSON, G., *An Essay on the Economics of Detribalization*, Rhodes-Livingstone Institute Paper, No. 5, 1941.
YESUFU, T.M., *An Introduction to Industrial Relations in Nigeria*, Oxford University Press, 1962.
ZOLBERG, A., *Creating Political Order*, Rand McNally, 1966.

Index

Abeokuta, 8, 12, 22, 41, 42
Adamson (case of the failed electrician), 70–72, 74, 75
Adebo (Wages and Salaries Review) Commission, 4, 150–51, 152, 161, 163, 166
Adebo Reports,
    quotations from, 152
    recommendations of, 152–53, 166
Ado Ekiti, 12, 22
agbekoya movement, 141, 188n
Agege
    commercial life at, 8, 9, 15, 18
    see also enterpreneurs
    description of, 8–9
    growth of, 8, 15, 22, 54–55
    Market, 8, 15, 36, 66
    Motor Road, 8
    Native Court, 36, 38
    population of, 1, 52
    social inequality in, 9, 53–55
    social organization in, 21–23, 181n
Ajegunle, 7
Akanale, International union president, 118–119, 123, 134
Akin (case of the successful motor mechanic), 72–74, 77
Akure, 22
Amin, S., 179n
Aminu (case of worker in conflict over saving), 63–64
Apapa Port, 38, 86, 111
Arrighi, G., 187–88n
articulation, between Town and Estate, 15, 16
Awori, 11, 66

Bailey, F.G., 143
Bankole, Champion union president, 119, 122, 123
Banton, M., 2, 179n
Bariga, 27
Bates, R.H., 184n
Beer, C.E.F., 188n
Benyon, H., 184n
Big Men, 9, 15, 53, 54, 142
blackleg, 100
bribery, 26, 31, 33, 35, 37, 71, 154, 166

career chart, of factory workers
    departures from, 60–61, 63–64, 65–67, 69, 74–75
    stages of, 58
casual employment, 24–25, 31–32, 59, 71
categorical relationships, 82–86
Champion, beer-producing factory, 99, 117
Chinoy, E., 182n

199

choices
  between careers, 12–14, 16, 46, 179n
  between income surplus disposal, 43–44, 77
  of spouse, 65, 66
class analysis, 14, 143–44
class consciousness, 105, 135
class sentiments
  in everyday life, 94–105
  and folk models, 95–96
class situation, 14, 17, 18, 81, 95, 174
clerks, *see* white-collar workers
clubs, of migrants, 41–43, 99
Cohen, A., 180n, 181n, 189n
Cohen, R., 2, 17, 172, 184n, 185n, 187n, 190n
Collins, P., 190n
competitive individualism, 23, 100, 142
contractors, 15, 50, 53

Decree 53, 124, 125, 126, 156, 157, 163, 165
Dennis, N., *et al.*, 182n, 184n

Ebute Metta Railway Compound, 86, 111
Egba, 11, 22, 28, 41, 64
Egbado, 11
Ekiti, 11
Elders, 27–28, 32, 36–37, 38, 42, 44–45
Elkan, W., 179n, 187n
Enahoro, Chief, 153, 154, 155, 160
encapsulation, 29
entrepreneurs, and entrepreneurship
  at Agege, 8–9, 15, 23, 52–55, 100
  personalized nature of, 54
  as reference points, 50–51, 55
  returns from, 53–54
  and wider inequalities, 141–43, 174–76
  in Yorubaland, 49–52
  see also self-employment
Enugu coalminers' strike, 172
Epstein, A.L., 1, 144, 179n, 184n, 187n
established workers
  definition of, 49
  incomes of, 49
  and savings, 57–69
  and self-employment, 57, 69–74
  trade union leaders as, 185n
ethnicity, 11, 22, 28, 29, 30, 186n
European companies, 4, 5, 16, 49, 59
  conditions of employment in, 25, 87, 89, 90–91, 92–94, 121–23
  description of, 6
  and government, 147–49, 161–62
  managements of, 96

folk-model, of workers, 95–96
foremen, *see* skilled workers
Fraenkel, M., 179n
friendships between migrants
  an entry to Town, 32
  ethnic content of, 28–29
  extent and range of, 28
  help exchanged within, 29, 37, 38
  and sanctioning, 42–43

General Strike of 1945, 172
General Strike of 1964, 101–2, 112–13, 123, 145, 150, 160, 170, 171, 172
Ghana, 2, 188n
Gluckman, M., 2
Grillo, R.D., 2, 182n, 184n, 187n, 188n

Index

Gutkind, P.C.W., 2, 189n

Harries-Jones, P., 2
Hausa, at Agege, 181n
Hoggart, R., 182n
home-town, 18, 21, 28
   and conflict, 61, 63
   and junior siblings, 62–63
   relationships with, 44, 61–67
   visits to, 40–41, 66
home-townsmen, *see* friendships and social networks
Hopkins, A.G., 172
house unions, *see* trade unions

Ibadan, 11, 43, 61, 67, 70, 141, 146
ideology,
   of brotherhood, 35
   of class and resistance, 95–102, 104
Ijebu, 11, 41, 59, 186n
Ijebu Ode, 12, 67, 72
Ijesha, 11
Ikeja Government Residential Area, 10, 46, 97, 140
Ikeja Housing Estate, 10, 97
Ikeja Industrial Estate
   description of, 1, 5–8
   employers on, 6
   location and area of, 1, 5–6
   products of, 6
   separation of factories in, 6, 110
   size of workforce on, 1
Ikoyi Island, 46, 140
Ilaro, 12
Ilesha, 22
Ilupeju Industrial Estate, 103, 158, 183n
industrial action
   background to, 150–53

   beyond Ikeja, 158
   course of, 153–60
   in early years, 112, 122–23
   illegality of, 125–26, 157, 165
   interpretation of, 162–67
   in non-European firms, 101
   violence in, 158–59
   workers' pragmatism in, 164–67
   workers' reliance on, 93–94, 107, 109
industrial sabotage, 98–99
inflation, 4, 12, 46, 68, 75, 124–25, 126, 136, 151, 167
International, textile factory, 117

Kano, 5, 141, 158
Kapferer, B., 2
Kilby, P., 189n
Krapf-Askari, E., 180n

Lagos
   and Agege location, 1, 8
   inequalities in, 10, 46, 78, 140–41, 146, 175
   inflation in, 125
   suburbs of, 27
Lloyd, P.C., 2, 178n, 180n, 189n
Lockwood, D., 183n
Lubeck, P., 188n, 190n
Luckham, R., 189n

Mabogunje, A.L., 188n
'management men', 83, 84, 85, 90, 97, 106
marriage, of workers, 28, 61
   costs incurred, 66–67
   and entrepreneurial ambitions, 65–67
   and established workers, 65–67
Marx, K., 96

Mayer, P., 180n
Michels, R., 17
migrants
  and career choices, 12–13, 179
  class situation of, 14
  employment problems of, 23–26
  social characteristics of, 10–14
Mitchell, J.C., 1, 177n, 180n, 183n, 187n
Morgan Commission, 112, 152, 170
Mushin, 27

national bourgeoisie, 140, 146–47, 149, 162
national labour congresses, 114, 127, 129, 133, 151, 170
  see also United Labour Congress and Nigerian Trade Union Congress
Nigeria
  inequalities in, 46, 78, 140–42, 145–50, 163, 175–76
  labour force of, 3, 149–50, 171–73
  recent political developments in, 3–4, 124–25, 145–50
Nigerian Employers' Consultative Association (N.E.C.A.), 153, 157, 159, 161
Nigerian Trade Union Congress (N.T.U.C.), 127
non-European companies, at Ikeja, 6, 25, 36, 58–59, 101, 155, 172

occupational stereotypes
  content of, 82–83, 183n
  functions of, 84–86
Ode Ondo, 12, 22, 28, 36, 37
oil, 148, 162
Oshogbo, 22
Otta, 66

Palmer, R., 188n
Papa Okun, 8
Parkin, D., 2, 180n
Parsons, N., 188n
paternalism, in Ikeja firms, 96
Peace, A.J., 179n, 181n, 190n
Peel, J.D.Y., 2, 189n
Peil, M., 2, 188n, 189n
political class
  description of, 145–46
  and expatriate employers, 147–49, 153, 157–58, 159, 161–62
  and national bourgeoisie, 146–47, 161–62
Port Harcourt, 5
prestige
  of Elders, 27, 38
  of self-employment, 49, 51–52, 53, 56–57, 75, 78
  of union leadership, 99–100, 132
  among urban Yoruba, 49, 51
  of wage-employment, 51–52, 56–57, 75, 84, 87, 90
proletarian culture, 17, 100, 139
  expressions of, 94–102
proletarianization, voluntary and involuntary, 77

railwaymen
  in East Africa, 2
  in Nigeria, 50, 86, 111, 172
rite de passage, of migrants, 33

Sandbrook, R., 17, 184n, 191n
self-employment
  capital requirements for, 68, 69, 70, 72
  failure in, 70–72, 74–75
  obstacles to, 57–67
  prestige of, 49, 51–52, 53, 56–

Index

57, 75, 78
workers' ambitions for, 13–14, 49–68
workers' moves into, 69–75
see also entrepreneurs
Shagamu, 12
shopfloor workers, 13, 16–17
   ambitions of, 13, 16, 49, 55
   and collective action, 92–94, 105–7
   disenchantment and cynicism amongst, 46, 76–79, 129, 140–41, 154, 156, 162–69
   and the government, 136, 167–69, 171, 173
   income levels of, 11, 24–26, 49
   job insecurity amongst, 15–16, 24–25
   political status of, 126–28, 136–37, 149–50, 162–69
   and pragmatism, 58, 75, 164–67
   relation to production, 14
   social characteristics of, 10–14
   stereotypes held by, 83
   stereotypes of, 82–83
   and the urban poor, 141–43, 174–76
   and wider inequalities, 46–47, 77–79, 140–43
   work and market situations of, 93–94
   see also migrants, established workers and trade unions
skilled workers, 10, 17
   backgrounds of, 86–87
   and entrepreneurship, 88–89, 183n
   incomes of, 87
   stereotypes held by, 82
   stereotypes of, 83–84
   stigma attached to, 93, 97–98
   and trade unionism, 90, 105–6
   work and market situations of, 87–88
Sierra Leone, 2
Smock, D.R., 187n
social mobility
   in Agege, 54–55
   in Ikeja factories, 86–87, 91–92
   in Yorubaland, 50, 52
social networks
   characteristics of, 29–30
   development and change in, 33–35, 38, 43, 59–60
   economies within, 30
   examples of, 180n
   income surplus in, 31–32, 33, 39–42
   reciprocity and trust in, 23, 32–35, 59
   residence of, 30
   sanctions within, 42–43
   as support units, 31, 36–39
strikes, *see* industrial action
Sule (case of the rebellious factory worker), 102–5

tailoring, 74, 75
target workers, 13, 187n
Thompson, E.P., 171
trade unions, 17–18, 25, 39, 40
   conflict within, 115
   democracy within, 119–121, 131, 155
   and Estate structure, 110, 135
   gains realized by, 121–23
   initial development of, 111–16
   internal organization of, 17–18, 119–21
   and labour congresses, 127, 128, 133–34

limitations of, 123–27, 128, 133, 135–36
meetings of, 120–21, 131, 155–56, 157, 160
politics within, 128–32
and shopfloor men, 92–94, 107, 109
teams within, 130
trade union leaders, 17, 99, 100
  as brokers, 131
  changes amongst, 114–16
  characteristics of, 112, 113, 116–19
  emergence of new men amongst, 114–16
  prestige of, 99, 130
  re-election of, 169
  and strike action, 116, 122, 126, 158–60, 164–65, 170–71
Touraine, A., 182n
transporters, 9, 15, 50, 53, 55
Tunde (case of the unstable Ondo migrant), 36–39

Uganda, 2
unemployment, 24, 31, 33, 34, 37, 44
United Africa Company, 86
United Committee of Central Labour Organizations (U.C.C.L.O.), 151, 154
United Labour Congress (U.L.C.), 127, 128, 133, 134
urban brothers, *see* social networks

van Onselen, C., 188n
Vincent, J., 189n

wage-earners,
  in private employment, *see* skilled workers, white collar workers, and shopfloor workers
  in public employment, 3, 55, 56, 144, 145, 150, 171, 172, 173
Weber, M., 96
Weeks, J., 189n
white collar workers, 17
  ambitions of, 91
  education of, 90
  incomes of, 91, 92
  and trade unionism, 92, 105, 106, 117–18, 158
  stereotypes held by, 83
  stereotypes of, 82–83
  work and market situations of, 91
Williams, G., 2, 189n
Wilson, G., 189n
work and non-work, separation of, 5, 6, 81

Yoruba kingdoms, 1, 11, 12, 22
Yorubaland
  entrepreneurship in, 49, 50
  social differentiation in, 49–50, 55

Zambia, 2
Zaria, 5

LIBRARY OF DAVIDSON COLLEGE

Books